DIDCOT STEAM
APPRENTICE

DIDCOT STEAM APPRENTICE

1960-66

PATRICK KELLY

· RAILWAY HERITAGE ·
from
The NOSTALGIA Collection

I dedicate this book to my grandsons
Charlie and Alex
This is how I enjoyed my life.
Love from Grampy xxx

First published in 2008

British Library Cataloguing in Publication Data

A catalogue record for this book is available from the British Library.

ISBN 978 1 85794 310 8

Silver Link Publishing Ltd
The Trundle
Ringstead Road
Great Addington
Kettering
Northants NN14 4BW

Tel/Fax: 01536 330588
email: sales@nostalgiacollection.com
Website: www.nostalgiacollection.com

Printed and bound in the Czech Republic

Frontispiece The front of Didcot shed, looking from the coal stage. The small building in the foreground is the sand-drying shed, beyond which is the office with its clock, which everybody worked from, then the range of different cabins or rest rooms. The Lifting Shop is at the end, and the roads on the left lead down to where the breakdown van was kept, and the turntable. Rising above the slate roof is the chimney of the Chargehand's stoves. Sometimes a young apprentice with energy to spare would walk along this roof and drop an out-of-date detonator down the chimney of a less popular Chargehand, but woe betide him if he was caught, as he would be sacked. *Author*

ACKNOWLEDGEMENTS

My thanks are due to the following people, without whose help I could not have worked on this book: Marion and Keith ('Bengy') Carter; Derek Everson (for help with photographs); Fenland Typewriter Services, King's Lynn; Sheila and Tony Neal (Didcot driver); Don Osbourne (Studio Atlanta, Didcot); Newsquest (Oxfordshire) Ltd; Bill Peto; *Reading Post*, Berkshire; Mrs Joyce Rowson and Mrs Maureen Darling; R. J. Russell (signalman, for help with photographs); Jimmy Tyler; Reg Warr and all at the GWR Retirement Club; Paul, my brother; and last but not least my wife Jennifer, for putting up with me.

CONTENTS

Introduction   7

1   1960: Fitter's boy   11
2   1961: Didcot apprentice   25
3   1962: Shed life   44
4   1963: Reading Diesel Depot   60
5   1964: Old Oak Common and Didcot: antics and accidents   75
6   1965: Swindon Works   93
7   1966: A Fitter at Oxford   108
8   Reunions   124

Index   127

NOTES ON DESCRIPTIONS OF STEAM LOCOMOTIVES

Steam locomotives are usually described in terms of their wheel arrangements, looking from the front. For example:

0-4-2   Four driving wheels with no wheels in front but two 'trailing' wheels behind

0-6-0   Six driving wheels only, with no wheels in front or behind

2-6-0   Two front wheels on a 'pony truck', six driving wheels, no wheels behind

2-6-2   Two front wheels on a 'pony truck', six driving wheels, two 'trailing' wheels

4-6-0   Four front wheels on a 'bogie', six driving wheels, no 'trailing' wheels

2-8-0   Two front wheels on a 'pony truck', eight driving wheels, no 'trailing' wheels

Tank locomotives, which carried their own coal in a bunker and water in tanks, are denoted by the addition of a 'T' after the wheel arrangement (eg 0-6-0T). 'T' denotes a side tank (tanks on each side of the boiler resting on the frames), 'PT' a pannier tank (with tanks suspended on each side of the boiler), and 'ST' a saddle tank (with a curved tank mounted on top of the boiler). Other engines had a separate tender (not included in the wheel arrangement) carrying larger quantities of coal and water, and were built for longer journeys.

The smaller wheels in front of and/or behind the driving wheels assist the locomotive in running round curves. The 2-6-2T 'Prairie' tanks have wheels in front and behind so can run as easily forwards or backwards. The bogie at the front of a 'Castle' 4-6-0, for example, does the same; such locos never run at speed in reverse, so need no trailing wheels.

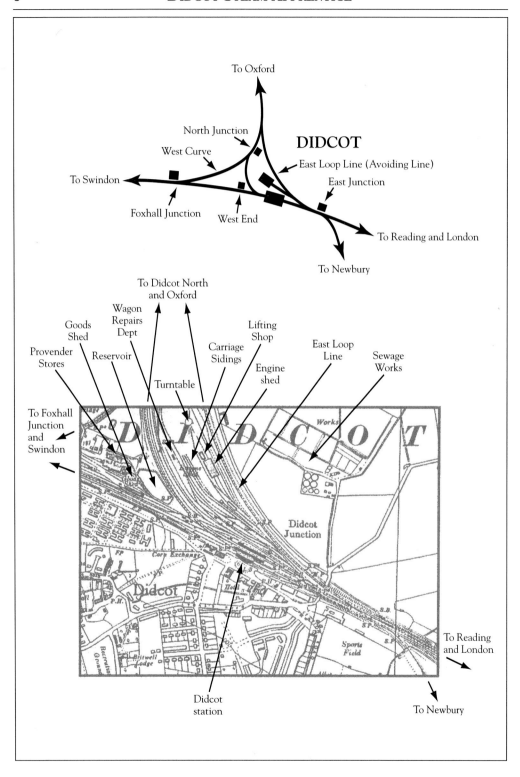

To Oxford

North Junction

West Curve

DIDCOT

East Loop Line (Avoiding Line)

To Swindon

East Junction

Foxhall Junction

West End

To Reading and London

To Newbury

To Didcot North
and Oxford

Wagon
Repairs
Dept

Goods
Shed

Lifting
Shop

Provender
Stores

Reservoir

Carriage
Sidings

East Loop
Line

Sewage
Works

Turntable

Engine
shed

To Foxhall
Junction
and
Swindon

Didcot
Junction

To Reading
and London

Didcot
station

To Newbury

INTRODUCTION

Didcot's place on the railway map came about by mistake. The original 1839 plan for the Great Western Railway was to travel from Reading to Abingdon, bypassing the rural village and many farms in the area, but the townspeople in Abingdon rejected the plans in Parliament, keeping the line away from Abingdon.

Isambard Kingdom Brunel built the first station at Didcot in 1852, made from wood, and plenty of it. In March 1866 it burned down; the fire is believed to have started in the Telegraph Office when a porter was filling a lamp with rape oil and he allowed some to spill over close to the office fire. In no time at all the whole station was well alight. Didcot had no fire brigade so a horse-drawn appliance had to be called from Harwell. On arrival it was quickly realised that they could not cope as the fire had got too good a hold, so they sent an emergency call by telegraph to Oxford for help from their appliance. Others came from Wallingford and Abingdon, and as darkness fell the huge flames, still shooting up high into the sky, could be seen from many miles away.

The new station was rebuilt to the same design as the first. Didcot grew with the help of the Army coming to the town, then, with a new marshalling yard, it became a junction, and passengers stayed over to await the next trains on their journeys, staying in the local hotel in front of the station. The Great Western Hotel was built in 1846, and renamed The Dragon Hotel in later years. The hotel next door was The Prince of Wales, built some time in the 1860s.

The Corn Exchange was built 1857, situated next to the railway line in Station Road nearly opposite Haydon Road. This was used to sell the local farmers' cattle and sheep, which were then herded onto the waiting trains. In later years it was used for the Permanent Way, and also the training of railway personal on First Aid Courses.

●

When I was 12 years old, coming home from a holiday in Ireland with my parents, we came off the ship at Fishguard Harbour and, after going through Customs, found the train waiting at the station. My Dad read the noticeboard: 'All passengers for Didcot please travel in the last carriage of the train'. This was the slip coach, and the train would not be stopping at Didcot, which was the changing point for several other stations – Newbury, Oxford, Cholsey – and all the small villages that had their own little stations before Dr Beeching came along and closed them. So, with all our bags and baggage we found a seat, although we were packed in like sardines in a can. These carriages never had a lot of room, so people often sat on their cases in the corridor.

The first carriage was slipped from a moving train in 1858 at Banbury in Oxfordshire, and Slough near London. The slip coach was attached to the last carriage of the train, with its own guard, and he would operate the controls when the time came to finally leave the main train. When the train pulled out of the station the next stop after Didcot would be Reading, then Paddington.

As the train got nearer to Foxhall signal box, west of Didcot, the driver of the steam locomotive applied the vacuum brake slightly to indicate to the guard, who was by then in his cab in the slip carriage, that the train was getting close to being disconnected. The guard would see his vacuum gauge needle drop or waver slightly, and this was the signal to begin the procedure to release the carriage from the main train. He would then push the slip lever forward, which would release the locking bolt on the coupling hook; the hook would drop forward and the driver of the locomotive would apply the vacuum brake once more. This would cause the slip carriage to buffer up to the rest of the train, and the coupling linkage would drop, in turn releasing the vacuum and steam heating pipes to drop into position, and not drag along the railway line. The slip carriage would then be free from the rest of the train, travelling on its own.

The slip guard, sitting in his cab, would now wind the brake lever slowly down, just enough so that the brake blocks touched the wheels, all the while keeping an eye on the distance to the station at Didcot. Applying the brake a bit harder, the carriage would enter the station, the guard sounding a bell on the front of the carriage to inform people that a train was coming in. Then it would stop, and everybody would get out of the carriage.

However, many a time the slip carriage would miss the platform, and travel on to the East signal box, and sometimes further on to Moreton marshalling yard, which was about 5 miles away – or wouldn't reach the station at all because the guard was too heavy on the brake lever. This meant that the station pilot locomotive would have to go out and bring in the slip carriage with all the people inside. Then hear the moans!

The quietness of the slip carriage could be

The 7.00am up Weston-super-Mare train detaching a slip carriage at 9.09am outside Foxhall signal box in 1950. *R. J. Russell*

dangerous. Between Didcot and Appleford the railway line ran through Hill Farm, whose land was on both sides of the line, so a level crossing was provided close to the farm, used by the farmer and his family between trains. When fog and winter weather conditions arrived, the farmer's son would lie on several sacks stuffed with hay close to the railway line with his ear pressed against the rail to listen for vibrations, allowing people to cross the level crossing in safety. On one particular day, after a train went by, the dung cart was pulled over the crossing; then the slip coach came into view, gliding down the railway line very quietly, and missed the dung cart by inches.

●

In 1958, when I was 13 years old, I went through a bad time. I got involved with two brothers, and when we were together we got 'too big for our boots' and nearly got my Dad the sack from what was still referred to then as the Great Western Railway, despite ten years since nationalisation.

The railway line to Newbury, Winchester and Southampton ran at the back of the houses where I lived in Didcot, in what was then the county of Berkshire (now Oxfordshire). It was used for passenger services and goods train, mostly to the docks at Southampton, and was also a short cut across the country, missing out Reading. In later years Dr Beeching came along and the line disappeared.

We three lads went down to a cattle crossing where some signals were located and started throwing stones around, causing a bit of damage. That evening the local policeman and the railway police came knocking at the door. I was in the bath, but I heard my Dad's voice in the kitchen and he was talking very loudly. I heard him say that he would sort out the problem. After Dad had spoken to the police, they left.

The next moment the bathroom door sprang open, a huge pair of hands came heavily down on my head and shoulders, and I was pulled vertically up out of the bath. I was then dragged into the bedroom. Around his waist Dad always wore a leather belt, and so did my backside that night. I was sent to bed with no dinner – nothing to eat or drink – just the pain from my backside and the strap marks. Dad sorted me out that evening, and kept his job at Didcot shed!

I went back to the St Birinus boys' school the next day and had another hiding from the two brothers. I was then taken into the Headmaster's office and given the cane for fighting.

●

Before leaving the boys' school two years later I was asked by my Dad what I would like to do as a career. We talked over the different aspects and ideas, and Dad asked me if I would be prepared to join the Great Western Railway at Didcot as an Apprentice Fitter and Turner. Both his other boys, Paul and Dick, where time-served Fitters and Turners, and Dad said he would like me to go with the same career. Then we talked about the prospects with different firms where I might work. Dad told me that the Great Western Railway would take on an apprentice as a Fitter and Turner, but he would have to enquire through the Didcot Shedmaster, who in turn would enquire at Paddington to see if a place was vacant for me at Didcot shed. In the days before 1960 the only way to get accepted onto the railway was if a relative or parent worked there.

After two to three weeks my Dad came back with the answer, and told me that I would be accepted for the position at Didcot Running & Maintenance Depot, starting as a Fitter's boy.

Then after a year, on my 16th birthday, I would have to sign the appropriate papers to become a full apprentice, and be trained as a Fitter and Turner.

When I returned back to school the following Monday morning, our class had a visit from the Careers Officer, and I was asked what I wanted to do. My reply was that my Dad had got me a position on the Great Western Railway.

Didcot's locomotive allocation in October 1959

0-6-0	0-6-0PT	5783	2-6-0	4-6-0 'Hall'
2214	1502	7772	2819	4913 *Baglan Hall*[1]
2221	3622	8435 (WB)	2836	4939 *Littleton Hall*
2234	3653	8458 (YE)	2844	4959 *Purley Hall*
2240	3709	9407 (NBL)	5326	4965 *Rood Ashton Hall*
2252	3721		5337	4969 *Shugborough Hall*
3210	3751	**0-6-2T**	5351	4994 *Downton Hall*[2]
3211	4649	5639	5380	5943 *Elmdon Hall*
	5744	5647	7324	6910 *Gossington Hall*
	5746 (NBL)		7327	6915 *Mursley Hall*
				6952 *Kimberley Hall*

All were Swindon-built except those marked NBL (North British Locomotive Co Ltd), WB (W. G. Bagnall Ltd) and YE (Yorkshire Engine Co Ltd).

4-6-0 'Modified Hall'
6969 *Wraysbury Hall*
6983 *Otterington Hall*[3]
6996 *Blackwell Hall*

[1] No 4913 came to Didcot from Reading shed on 4 November 1959
[2] No 4994 left Didcot shed in October 1959
[3] No 6983 went to Swindon for repairs in October 1959

The team at Didcot Running & Maintenance Shed, 1960

Foreman
Arthur Brinkley

Fitters
Jim Tyler – Lifting Shop Fitter
Dave Davis
Ted Powell
Burt Passey
Norman Brogden
Paul Kelly
Bob Looms
Jim Holmer
Jack Dearlove

Fitters' mates
Jim Hale
Frank Dowding
Matt Oglesby
Bob Warrick
Charlie Clanfield

Office Clerk
Sam Morgan

The front of Didcot shed on a cold morning – note the white frost on the sleepers. The building on the right is the sand store. *Author*

1
1960: FITTER'S BOY

I left St Birinus School at Didcot at Easter 1960. I was 15 years old in February of that year, and my home was 28 Sinodun Road, Didcot (named after the Sinodun Hills that overlooked the River Thames near Wallingford).

Before starting work on my first morning I had to finish my paper round for Don Avery, the newsagent at the bottom of Station Road. I had to sort my own papers with addresses before going out to deliver them, and collect the paper money. My pay for the week (including Saturday) was 15s 6d.

That first Monday morning I started work at 8.00am at Didcot Running Shed as a Fitter's boy. As you entered the shed, on the left-hand side were the offices along No 1 road. First were the offices of the Shedmaster, George East, and the Shed Foremen, then followed the Time Clerk's office, the lobby room and time desk – where the drivers picked up information about train schedules – the stores hatch, the stores main door, the drivers' and firemen's mess room, the Foreman Fitter's office, the Fitters' mess room, the Boilersmiths' mess room, the Shedmen's mess room, the Cleaners' mess room, and finally the WC and shower room. Then came the huge double doors to the Lifting Shop, with a small door for access. At the end of the shop's full-length inspection pit were more doors, giving access to the shed yard. There were eight roads around the shed, plus two going down to the turntable. One of these was used for the breakdown van, with a standby locomotive on at all times.

First I had to report to the Shedmaster, Mr East, in his office at the main entrance to the shed, where I was given a brass disc, which was to be my pay number while I worked there – the number was 388. Then I was introduced to Mrs Bray, the time clerk, and was told how the system worked – 7.30am start and 5.30pm finish, with an hour for lunch, five days a week plus a Saturday morning. The pay was £1 10s 0d for a 48-hour week; I gave my Mum £1 and had the 10 shillings for myself. I was told that every year, after completing a year's service, I would have a pay rise of £1. I was taught the safety side of things, like not to jump the pits, to stop, look and listen for steam locomotives, and whenever the weather was bad to be on my guard. I was given a safety book to read, and was then introduced to Mr Arthur Brinkley, the Workshop Foreman.

Arthur took me out of the pay clerk's office and we both walked down towards the Lifting Shop. As we walked along he explained the running shed to me. He showed me his office, and the mess cabin where I was to have my meals. I also met all the staff on duty, was shown where to put my clothes, and was issued a locker with a key for my personal items; this was also the place where I would keep my teapot, cup, sugar and tea. The locker room was very cold in the winter, as there was no heating. Outside, in the Lifting Shop, there was a long ceramic trough hand basin with overhead pipes feeding hot and cold water into the taps to wash our hands.

At that time my whole family worked on

Above Didcot coaling stage in 1967. *Author*

Left 0-6-0PT 'tanky' No 8720 on Road 4 at Didcot shed, looking across to the ash pan area on the left. *Author*

the railway. My Mum was a Carriage Cleaner, cleaning the insides and the corridors, at Didcot Carriage Sidings. My Dad, Chris Kelly, worked on the coal stage, where he would shovel coal from the coal wagons that were pushed up the slope a few at a time by a 'tanky', 0-6-0T No 3721 or No 3751. He would then shovel the coal into a trolley, which had four cast-iron wheels and held 10 quintal (hundredweight) of coal. This was then pushed onto a ramp hanging over the locomotive tender and tipped over the edge. The height from the ground to the trolley ramp was about 15 feet.

Other railways raised the coal in wagons to a great height, then tipped the load into the tender far below, but this could not be done on the Great Western as they used soft Welsh Steam Coal, which would be broken by that method.

Mum and Dad got up each morning at 4.30am, had breakfast together, then walked to work for 6.00am. Later Dad transferred to the shed as a Boilerman with Trevor May, washing the scale and muck from the boilers through the 'mud hole' doors – the scale was caused by the hard water in the Great Western area.

My eldest brother Paul had just finished his National Service in the Royal Navy, and completed his apprenticeship at the REME workshops at Didcot Ordnance Depot; he then started at Didcot Running Shed as a Fitter and Turner, which was his trade. He was eight years older than me. My other brother Richard (Dick) was time-served on the Great Western at Didcot; he was also a Fitter and Turner, but when he completed his time in 1958/59 he transferred to Oxford as a Fitter. Dick was a year younger than Paul. Even to this day, when I visit the Railway Staff Club the old railwaymen call us the 'Family of Fitters'.

During the day I worked alongside my Dad and we were mates together, but at home he was my Father, and the man of the house. I was still young enough to feel his belt and I did a few times – I had a job to sit down with the bruises for two or three days afterwards.

I was put with a chap called Jimmy Tyler, and the only way to describe him was that he was as strong as an ox! He was always working in the Lifting Shop, stripping out the

locomotives, removing axles, side-rods, connecting-rods, pistons and valves. The first steam locomotive I worked on was 4-6-0 No 6953 *Leighton Hall*. Jimmy stood next to it and showed me that the centre driving wheels were out on the floor near the lathe. The wheels were hooked on to a straight lifting bar with the ends turned upwards, which went through the spokes; this was then hooked on to the swing-away crane. The loco looked odd with the wheels missing and a big gap with nothing there – a 4-4-0 rather than a 4-6-0!

In fact, the GWR once owned a 4-5-0 locomotive! In 1930 the left-hand leading driving wheel came off 'Saint' Class 4-6-0 No 2933 *Bibury Court* as she was approaching Olton near Birmingham at 70mph. It rolled down the embankment and the driver, with great care, brought the train to a stand.

Jimmy wiped his hands with some sort of cotton waste, then took me under the locomotive; I was told to keep my head down, because in those days there were no hard hats for protection – we only had a miner's helmet with a lamp fixed to it, and a belt around your waste to which the battery was attached.

I was shown the connecting-rod (con-rod), a long piece of square bar tapered slightly at one end where it was attached to the crosshead, which was driven back and forth by the piston. At the other end there was a round brass bush fixed onto the journal, which in turn was fitted into the con-rod. This would then be fitted with a large nut with two flat sides, turned by an oval spanner; with the help of a sledge hammer banging down on the spanner, the oval nut would be driven round to expose the fixing hole, in which a long bolt and nut could be tightened up. Then a split pin would be knocked into a hole in the bolt, and its legs opened. The con-rod would then be put onto the middle driving wheel. In Swindon Works these con-rods where hand-filed by apprentices and Fitters' mates after they came out of the foundry.

We smelted and remoulded white metal, which we got from the stores as 'ingots'. I was taught how to mix the moulding clay, not too wet, and would clear a space on the forge corner. While we were mixing the clay, a ladle was set into the fire on the forge. Gripped by

Left No 6953 *Leighton Hall* outside the lifting shop in 1960 waiting for its centre driving wheels. *R. J. Russell*

Right The set of driving wheels and journal boxes inside Didcot's Lifting Shop. Note the equipment ranged along the far wall of the workshop. *R. J. Russell*

Below Another loco with driving wheels missing is No 5985 *Mostyn Hall,* seen outside the shed at Didcot. It is waiting for the wheels and axle boxes to come from Swindon Works. On the right is 9F No 92227. *R. J. Russell*

prongs, an 'ingot' was laid into the ladle, where it soon ran like molten lava, and with a flat iron bar Jimmy would scrape the waste off the top, to stop any dirt forming in the bearing, and also to stop the white metal blowing back at us.

Also with us was a chap called Norman, who was not long out of his apprenticeship. He thought it funny to melt a white metal 'ingot' then drop it into a water trough next to the forge till the water boiled with the heat from the molten liquid, but it flew back at his body, slightly burning him.

The bearings were in two halves, which were bolted together with the huge nuts and bolts. I was shown how to mould the clay around the bearing. Then we measured the size of the journal on the axle of the wheel with the outside callipers, or 'odd legs'. There were round iron bushings spare in the Lifting Shop cupboard, especially made in Swindon for this work. Finding the right size, the bush was fitted inside the middle of the bearing, and the molten white metal poured very carefully inside the bushing, and the outside of the iron round the bushing. As soon as the metal had cooled off, the new bearing was pushed off the forge onto the floor, then the iron bushing was removed with prongs back to the cupboard. This was done twice, as there were two sets of bearings to each set of wheels.

With the help of two other men the completed bearing had to be lifted up onto the lathe, fixed into the lathe chuck and tightened down. Then the bearing was turned to the size of the axle journal, measuring it frequently with the 'odd legs'; again, this had to be done twice. The new metal bearings where then split into two halves, and I was shown how to scrape them out to fit the axles of the driving wheels.

This was the hard part. Using engineer's blue or red paste spread thinly on the driving wheel axle, we would find the high spots on the bearing sliding around the axle, then, with a special tool, we would scrape out the bearings for days and days until they fitted on the set of driving wheels. It was precision work, requiring precise filing and scraping out of the oil traps and channels. It was also wearisome work.

The Lifting Shop also had its own tools,

which were standard in all depots. The general technique involved a motor pulling a lever to move a belt. The lever would slide a pulley into place to drive another belt, which would then allow you to operate lathes, drilling machine and grinding machine.

We also had a hoist crane with a maximum lift of 50 tons, which was made by Royce of Manchester and installed in 1932 for lifting locomotives up at the leading end or the cab end. This was only done when the tender was removed. To operate the crane you would first lift off the cover in which the gearing cogs were kept and make sure that it was in low gear by putting your hand in to slide the cog across to the left. Then, by lifting the brake handle and pressing a green button, it would begin to operate. When you heard the crane take the strain, down came the brake handle to shut off the motor, then the gearing cog was pushed across away from you into the lowest gear. Then up came the brake again and you pushed the green button to start the lift, replacing the cover over the gears. Once lifted, the locomotive was 'blocked' with square blocks of wood, so you could climb underneath to do your work. These blocks of oak were approximately 3 feet square and 6 to 8 feet long, and were very heavy with years of grease and oil stains embedded in them.

I got on well with Jimmy. After a few months the oxygen and acetylene bottles became empty and needed changing, so we went to the stores, about 50 yards away, to see if there were any spares. Jimmy carried the empty acetylene bottle on his shoulder, although it was heavy, and I picked up the empty oxygen bottle in the same way; we brought the full ones back from the stores on a barrow.

Part of a Fitter boy's job was tea-making. I had to go to Midwinter's shop outside the station next to The Old Tap, which was a run-down and dirty pub. Midwinter's was a lovely shop with different smells and a wooden floor that creaked when you walked on it. It never seemed to close, and sold everything: cakes, veg, fruit, papers, tins of everything, and bottles of Corona pop with screw lids. The lids had wire attached to them so that when you opened the bottle you didn't lose the lid.

Left A view of the footplate of preserved GWR 4-6-0 No 4079 *Pendennis Castle* in the Lifting Shop, showing the controls. The regulator lever, controlling the valve that admits steam to the cylinders, is on the left; its long handle has a counterweight at the top end. To the right of the regulator is the vacuum brake – the round disc with the lever at the top pointing to the right. The two-handled wheel on the right is the reversing gear; it is wound to the right (clockwise) to go forward, to the left (anti-clockwise) to go in reverse. On the extreme right above the gear control is the Automatic Train Control bell, which indicates to the driver whether signals ahead are clear or not, different sounds being used in each case. At the bottom left of the photo are the firebox doors, opened and closed by the lever with the chain. On top of the firebox opening is a shelf, carrying a lamp to the left, then a billycan containing the crew's tea, kept hot on the shelf. *Author*

Below Pendennis Castle in the Lifting Shop, seen through the 'A' frame carrying the crane wire drum and control box. The large wheel on the right with elongated holes cut in it is the brake system. A white cloth is laid on the motor, next to which is the gearing box that controls the crane. The lifting capacity in low gear was 50 tons. *Author*

Above The smokebox and chimney of *Pendennis Castle* in the Lifting Shop. *Author*

Above Another view, giving some idea of the height of the footplate from the ground. *Author*

Below No 4079's motion and driving wheels. A buffer spring stands in the foreground. *Author*

I was easy prey to practical jokers when I left school. Gullible is the word. One day I was sent across to Midwinter's shop for ¼lb of tea, ½lb of sugar, some skyhooks and a tin of vacuum. The shop was full of people and the owner, Mr Midwinter, kept telling me he hadn't got anything like skyhooks or vacuum in his shop – he also told me that I had been 'had'. On my way back to work I found an old tin with the top missing, but I couldn't find any skyhooks. I had the mickey taken out of me something rotten, but I gave the tin to the chap who sent me and told him the vacuum was already been sucked out of it.

Another job was to wash the Fitter's tools on a Friday afternoon, as they became covered in coal dust and grease. I would go to the stores for a bucket of paraffin and cotton waste, sign the stores book to show what was taken, then walk back to the Lifting Shop, put all the tools in the bucket a few at a time, which would prevent the paraffin overflowing on the floor, then make sure that they were wiped clean, and that there were no metal offcuts in the cotton waste. (The cotton waste came in bulk bales, and was made by prisoners across the country; sometimes pieces of metal would be found inside it.) Then I had to replace the tools in their correct position every Friday afternoon in the Fitter's tool cabinet.

In the summer of 1960 another Fitter's boy started. He had also gone to St Birinus School at Didcot, and his name was Keith Benjamin

Paul Carter, nicknamed 'Bengy'. Bengy stayed with me through the years; I was just a bit older than he was and when I moved to a new depot he followed a year later.

Bengy and myself were rogues when we were together. The summer of 1960 was very hot, and many years later, while writing this book, Bengy nudged my memory of events. In our team of Fitters was a chap named Bob Looms. We called him Belgian Bob, because he had been a Spitfire pilot in the Second World War – well, that's what he told Bengy and me. He always wore the RAF badge on his sports jacket pocket. Bob was quiet, and always drank his tea strong and sweet. He lived in the Railway Hostel near the Railway Staff Club.

One day we had a locomotive on No 2 road in the shed, a 'Grange' Class 4-6-0. (No 1 road was mostly kept clear because it led into the Lifting Shop; if there was a locomotive on it, it would be ready to go out, all fired up.) Two teams of two were working on the locomotive, a Fitter and his mate on one side, and Bob and his mate on the other. They had to strip out and take off the con-rods and crosshead, the front piston plates, and the linkages for the valves. The idea was to fit new piston rings and valve rings because steam was leaking past them, so there was no compression and no drive. The other team finished and refitted their side back together correctly, while our Bob and his mate also put all the parts back in

Didcot apprentices in 1962: myself ('Wobble') (*below*) and Keith Carter ('Bengy'). *Author*

Right   The overflow Railway Hostel huts in Station Road, Didcot. *R. J. Russell*

Below On No 2 road at the front of the shed is No 6922 *Burton Hall*. Working on No 1 road is shed cleaner Dick Bidmead, cleaning out the pit of ashes. *Author*

Left and middle Views of a 'Hall' Class piston, crosshead and connecting rods. The locomotive is at Didcot awaiting repairs in 1960. *Author*

Left A 'WD' Class motion and piston. *Author*

Didcot's locomotive allocation in November 1960

0-6-0	2-6-0	2-6-2T	2-8-0	4-6-0 'Hall'
2201	5351	6109	2819	4902 *Aldenham Hall*
2221	5380	6113	2836	4915 *Condover Hall*
2230	6302	6120	2839	4939 *Littleton Hall*
2240	6313	6124	2849	4950 *Patshull Hall*
	6363	6136	3211	4959 *Purley Hall*[2]
0-6-0PT	6379	6139		4965 *Rood Ashton Hall*
1502[1]	7324	6156		4969 *Shugborough Hall*
3622	7327	6159		4876 *Warfield Hall*
3653				5918 *Walton Hall*
3751				5943 *Elmdon Hall*
4649				5987 *Brocket Hall*
5746 (NBL)				6910 *Gossington Hall*
8720 (BP)				6915 *Mursley Hall*
				6937 *Conyngham Hall*

4-6-0 'Modified Hall'

All were Swindon-built except those marked NBL (North British Locomotive Co Ltd) and BP (Beyer Peacock Co Ltd).

6969 *Wraysbury Hall*
6983 *Otterington Hall*[3]

[1] Outside-cylinder 0-6-0PT No 1502 was built at Swindon in 1949, and placed in store from 16 June 1960. She had a short wheelbase and was able to travel over the uneven, sharply curved lines in the Central Ordnance Depot. When I saw her outside on Road 7 she was awaiting her fate, with sacking covering the chimney. Someone had left a bunch of wild flowers stuck into the smokebox door, and on the side of her water tank someone had written 'GOODBYE OLD GIRL' in large chalk letters. She was another sad example of a working locomotive going to the scrapyards at Barry in South Wales. However, she was later saved and sold from Swindon to the National Coal Board in 1961, to work for a few more years at Coventry Colliery until 1970, when she was eventually sold for scrap.

[2] No 4939 went to Swindon for repairs in November 1960

[3] No 6983 went to Swindon for repairs in October 1959

No 3721 moved on to Lydney on 4 November 1960

0-6-0PT No 3709 worked in the Central Ordnance Depot at Didcot; the spark arrestor fitted to the chimney allowed the engine to work inside sheds when shunting. *R. J. Russell*

the way that they thought was right. Bob oiled up all the bushes, then the shed fireman lit the fire and got the locomotive fired up overnight. With a full head of steam, the shed driver took the locomotive out, but it went out with a limp, like a person walking along a kerb with one foot on the road. It was brought back and Jimmy fixed it, then out it went the correct way. Bob only spoke in Belgian when he was raging.

When we started as Fitters' boys, the other trades, Fitters and their mates, started to fool about. Hanging up on the crane hoist was what looked like an 'A' frame, just a piece of flat wood tied to a rope, which was used for hanging and drying out the fire hoses. One day it was lowered down – approximately 15 feet – and Bengy sat on the plank, held on to the rope and was pulled, as on a Bosun's Chair, up into the gantry. Then he was lowered and it was my turn, so up I went, but this time they tied up the rope and started to walk away. I didn't like heights at the best of times, and was frightened to hell. They returned and started to lower me down, then they let it drop quickly and stopped it with a jolt. I was then lowered to the floor but I squashed two fingers in the pulley wheel because I held on so tightly. Never again would I go up on that chair, but Bengy loved it.

I was working in the Lifting Shop one afternoon and was being shown how to hold a chisel to sharpen it – I was told never to use the side face on the stone, but only the front face. The Fitter, Dave Davis, started up the motor to drive the belts, then pulled the lever into drive and away went the grinding stone. Well, there I was, goggles on, chisel being sharpened, when I noticed that the vice was slipping back, and the chisel jammed the stone to the vice. Someone grabbed me and pulled me to the ground, waiting for the stone to explode, but with luck it just jammed up. Dave shut off the motor, and when I looked at the chisel there was a fair lump taken out. After that I was very careful with grindstones.

Bengy and I liked to have a bit of fun together, so one afternoon we went into the shed's shower room and WC. We were messing about with the water and we flooded the room. I know I went home soaked to the

skin, and so did Bengy – but we didn't know what had happened till we were summoned to the Shedmaster's office the next morning and was told that there was a river flowing out of the WC. We were both threatened with the sack because two drivers had gone into the shower room that night and caused uproar about the mess. This was one of our many adventures throughout our apprenticeship. We went back into the shower room and cleaned it until it was spotless – I just didn't know where all the dirt and water had come from. George East came down and inspected the area and we both got a hell of a telling-off. But it was clean now.

Two inches of snow fell on 23 December, which was churned into slush by the traffic, and a freak storm caused power failures. But work on the Great Western went on as normal. On the morning of Christmas Eve I slept in and was late for work. Bengy and I had to clean out the Lifting Shop, the old wooden blocks on the floor and the inspection pit. There was a newspaper in the pit, but as I grabbed it to throw it away, something moved underneath it. I shouted to Bengy to grab one of the big heavy spanners hanging on the wall. As I pulled up the paper Bengy threw the spanner – the result, a squashed flat rat.

When we finished off our cleaning and tool work we were called into the mess room where all the Fitters and mates were. Then in came 'Brink' (Arthur Brinkley) and Sam Morgan, the Office Clerk. It was Christmas, and carols were what they wanted to hear, so to our surprise Bengy and I had to stand on the mess room table and sing our hearts out. This was apparently a tradition for apprentices and they had to do it. So we did, then the others opened the door and a few drivers and firemen came in to sing with the rest of the workshop staff. Everyone joined in and we had a good time together. Afterwards they gave us the collection in which all the men had put a coin and wished us a Merry Christmas. It was nice.

Bengy and I rode up to Smallbone's shop on The Broadway, which sold tobacco and sweets and ornaments, and bought a brass-handled bottle-opener in the shape of a naked lady for Brink and wished him a Merry Christmas! I then went to the Railway Staff Club to pick up my allotted ration of beer and Babychams, which is what we had every year, then soon Christmas was gone and Boxing Day too.

Next to the Fitters' cabin was the Boilersmiths' cabin. On nights two men would be on duty, the Smithy and his mate: Alan was the Smithy, Johnny his mate. Johnny would always come on duty early and get the pot-belly stove fired up and burning, then go to his locker, pull out a brand new clean metal bucket and lid, fill it full of water, and put it on the stove. He would then peel a few potatoes and drop them into the bucket, then out of his shoulder bag came a greaseproof paper bag containing two or three pig's trotters, which he dropped into the pot with a few cabbage leaves as extra. He would then go out to work with the Boilersmith, and when suppertime came the two of them came back into the cabin, and Johnny would give the bucket a stir with a wooden spoon, then put a big heap on his plate and refit the lid. When the day shift came in for their turn of duty, Johnny would put the bucket of stew in his locker with the lid on till the next night shift. Meanwhile, Alan, before going off duty in the morning, would shave, wash and clean up. He didn't have a normal shaving brush, but a soft pastry brush to get more lather on his face. Next night, in would come Johnny, out came the stew, off with the lid, scrape the fat off the top and onto the red-hot pot-belly stove.

One night two men were in the oil stores on No 1 road, and one had a fit, grabbed the pot-belly stove's metal chimney with both his hands and would not let go, although there was a full fire burning.

During my first year, when I heard a train going by outside near No 8 road on the Reading to Oxford loop, bypassing Didcot station, I would run out to watch it and see what the locomotive was. Everything went by rail then, and often there would be long 'Macaw' bogie bolsters, sometimes whole train lengths of maybe ten or more carrying heavy equipment. These wagons were designed to carry steel girders, or Army vehicles, tanks and

'Austerity' 2-8-0 No 90258 stored at Didcot in 1963. Note the wooden block to stop the engine rolling. *Author*

trucks. Army trains, with 'EXPLOSIVES' painted on the van sides, had their own service personnel, and sometimes we saw these men riding in the guard's van. If the train was stopped at signals for a while, the servicemen would check the wagons, making sure that there were no axles boxes running hot, checking each in turn. If there was a 'hot box' the whole train would have to be shunted into the marshalling yard, and the affected vehicle split away, which then had to be unloaded.

Loaded oil tank wagons were always marshalled at the rear of the train as far away as possible from sparks from the locomotive; these trains would have a box van or the guard's van connected up behind the tender. The fullest trains were banana trains, which ran regularly towards Birmingham from London, where Fyffes had their own warehouse. Sometimes we saw old red London Underground trains being towed by a locomotive either for scrap or to private companies for repair. Working these trains would be Churchward 'Moguls', 'Halls' and 'Granges', or 'Austerity' 90xxx 2-8-0s.

The Riddles-designed War Department 'Austerity' 2-8-0s and 2-10-0s were introduced in 1943 and purchased by British Railways in 1948. The locomotive weighed 70 tons 5 cwt and the tender 55 tons 10 cwt, and only 153 were built. They were mostly used for heavy freight work, and would sometimes pull coal trains up from South Wales. There were not a lot on the Western Region, but they were distinctive due to the clanging noise from their motions when moving along. I liked them because of this, and I also liked the shape and the movement of the con-rods. I remember seeing them stored at Didcot shed outside on No 7 road. One, No 90258, had her wheels scotched with wooden blocks from the railway line. They were eventually taken away and scrapped.

2
1961: DIDCOT APPRENTICE

It remained cold, but on 13 January the snow receded. We started getting very dirty each day, and the dirt got into the pores of our skin and was very difficult to get out. There was no Swarfega or hand cream then – the only way we could get them clean was to go across to the carriage and wagon breaker's yard and collect horsehair that had been used to stuff the cushions in the old coaches. This we would scrub into our hands and arms with carbolic soap; we also used soft soap and sand. We would then dry ourselves and dip our fingers in some gear oil (which was used for the oiling points on locomotive con-rods) and rub it in to our arms and hands. We got this tip from the 'old hands' like Ted Powell and Frank Dowding, and I can honestly say that I never had any trouble keeping my hands clean since then.

My Mum washed all the trousers and shirts for Dad, Dick and myself. We came home covered with dirt, grease, coal and dust. I would undress to my underpants in the scullery, then go straight upstairs for a bath with soda crystals in the water, and scrub myself with carbolic soap. My Mum had a very hard job washing our clothes; like most railwaymen we took our Mums for granted, but on Monday there were always clean clothes waiting for us. We only had a back boiler in the fire grate, so the fire was always lit. This was the case while I was stationed at Didcot – when I moved to other depots in later years, it all changed because the facilities got much better.

Some mornings, when leaving home, I would meet Bengy at Don Avery's at the bottom of Station Road, and we would ride in together on our bikes. We would race along Station Road and up over the kerb between Harold's and Priors Taxis, coming out into the station, then down through the tunnel where we were shouted at to 'Get off our bikes and walk!', so we would, and skate down on the pedals!

At the bottom, past the lifts, we would run up the stairs with our bikes on our shoulders, then cross the crossing. If we were lucky a train would be being shunted back into the carriage sidings. Other shed staff would be waiting on both sides to cross. We would belt like mad as soon as the locomotive allowed a clear view across the crossing, again hearing shouts and screams to slow down. We would race down the cinder track, weaving in and out of the other men, until we reached the cycle racks at the shed. Sometimes the Shed Foreman would approach us and then we had a reprimand. If we fell off, which I did a few times, we lost the skin from our hands and knees, and you had to be careful, as carriages were close to the path and many times we would clip a carriage and fly off our bikes. Fortunately we fell on cinders, not on concrete. When the shed was built in 1932 many wagonloads of ashes were brought from all over the London Division of the Great Western Railway to make a dry and level foundation for the new works, and in some places the ash is now 25 feet deep.

A six-wheeled clerestory-roofed coach in the carriage sidings at Didcot in 1950. The path to the shed is next to the railway line in the foreground. *R. J. Russell*

●

When wagons came off the road at North Moreton marshalling yard, about 3 miles away, we were often called out. The shed standby locomotive was ready coupled to the breakdown van and guard's van, with a driver and fireman available. Two standby men, a Fitter and his mate, were left on the shed were just in case locomotives came in off the main line requiring repair work.

The Foreman, with at least ten men and two Fitters' boys, went out in the breakdown van. When the men wanted tea, Bengy and I fired up the stove and, when it was roaring away, on went the old metal kettle, which was soon boiling. The tea-leaves went into the pot, milk in the mugs, sugar on the side, and it was brewed to perfection. Suddenly there was a shout. 'I can taste paraffin!' said Frank Dowding, and a couple more said the same. Bengy and I had forgotten to wash our hands. One man nearly lost his false teeth shouting at us.

The breakdown crew were paid an extra retainer for going out when vehicles came off he road. Sometimes they would be out all night and all day, and food would be brought to them. It was very tiring, pulling traverse jacks and blocks of timber around in all weathers, and crawling under a wagon or locomotive was frightening because you knew it could slip and drop on you. Until 1906 locomotives carried their own hydraulic jacks and drivers and firemen were expected to deal with minor derailments.

On returning to the shed after a derailment the Fitter's mate who was in charge of the breakdown van and the guard's van coupled to it had to gather all the stocks and provisions, the biscuits, tinned meats and tinned milk, and the coal and firewood for the stove, then, with help from Bengy or myself, climb up on the roof of the breakdown van by a ladder to refill the main water tanks with a hose. Then we would walk through into the store area where the jacks and the oils were kept. All the lifting jacks and traversing jacks had to be replenished with oil, ready for the next derailment, and the timber blocks stacked tidily in their own space.

One day the Shedmaster passed on a message from the main office at the marshalling yard, to get the shed driver and fireman down to the locomotive to couple up the breakdown van as another crash had happened in the yard. Brink, the Foreman, instructed the Fitters and mates to climb up into the breakdown van and get out of the shed as quickly as they could with help from the other shed staff, who went out to pull the points so that the breakdown train had a clear run up to the main line access signal. There the fireman climbed down from the footplate, opened the telephone box and called the signalman in the East Junction signal box, who duly changed the points, cleared the signal and allowed the small train out on to the main line.

Arthur Brinkley was in charge of the operation, and all orders came from him. He

Right Off the road: this tender has crashed into the buffers at the back of the Lifting Shop. *R. J. Russell*

Right A breakdown crew working to get a Pannier tank back on the line somewhere in the Oxford area. *Author*

Below Didcot East Junction signal box. The operating floor had 152 levers, and the box was rated as a Special C Class. Signalman Jack Gough is in attendance. *R. J. Russell*

inspected the situation. An empty wagon with fixed axles had jumped off the road after being loose-shunted, had come into contact with a few box vans, and bounced back with a crash. The driver got the breakdown van as close as possible, which helped the Fitters and their mates to carry the equipment, the traverse and lifting jacks and blocks of wood. Sometimes, if the track was in need of replacement, the breakdown van, like other derailment crews, carried its own rails. On many occasions the crew could not get near enough, so the equipment became heavy with all the walking and stepping in between the sleepers with great care. Also, when working in a marshalling yard care had to be taken because of the proximity of other moving trains – it was a dangerous place to be.

The Foreman ordered that the timber should be placed under the centre of the wagon that was off the road, with a stationary jack on top near the coupling hook. At the other end the traverse jack would be placed on top of some timber, then the stationary jack would be pumped up above the railway line. At the other end, where the traverse jack was, the wheels were blocked with wood, which stopped the wagon from moving. Next Arthur ordered that the traverse jack be pumped up above the railway line, then ratcheted sideways so that the wagon started to move back towards the line.

The stationary jack was then slowly lowered and two men brought in another traversing jack, which was placed where the stationary jack had been; again, the order was given to jack up above the rail, then ratchet the jack sideways in the opposite direction. The two traversing jacks worked in tandem, and the wagon was soon back above the rails. Both jacks were then lowered down onto the line.

The job done, Bengy and I were told to get into the breakdown van while the men brought the equipment back; as they lifted it up into the van we pulled it into position. Meanwhile the kettle was put on for tea or coffee and biscuits.

The driver then rang the signalman from the shunters' office opposite Didcot station, to get clearance to move the train back onto the main line and return to the shed. The wagon was pulled into the breaker's yard to see if any repair was needed.

●

On 25 February 1961 my Dad and I had to go to London to see Mr E. C. Bourne, the District Running & Maintenance Officer for Paddington, London, at the BR headquarters at 222 Marylebone Road. This was my big day, as I had to sign my apprenticeship papers. I had managed the first part – now I had to prove myself. My Dad was as pleased as Punch and shook my hand, but he did ask me there and then if I would promise him something. He asked me not to get married if I found someone before I finished my trade. I promised that I would do what he said, and he was over the moon! Then we went by Underground to Whitechapel to see my Aunt Betty and Uncle Mick – we had a free pass each, so it didn't cost us anything for the journey, and we had a great day out together.

●

When my brother Paul joined the railway, after a few weeks of completing several shifts working days and nights on a temporary basis he was ready for permanent shift work, seven days on or seven nights on, 12-hour shifts, 8.00pm until 8.00am, starting on Saturday night first shift, and ending Saturday morning. It was the same for all the Fitters and their mates. He was paid for 112½ hours, made up of double time, time and a half, and time and a third.

One morning in March 1961 there was a telephone call to the shed from Foxhall signal box. The Fishguard passenger boat train was limping into Didcot station, and could someone proceed to the station as the locomotive was in trouble.

Paul waited with his mate Bob on the correct London-bound platform and the 'Castle' Class locomotive coasted in, steam rising all around the boiler from the piston on the left-hand side. People were looking out of the carriage windows, wondering why the express train was moving so slowly into the

The piston rod and crosshead of a 'Castle'. It was the vertical bars to the right of the crosshead on the failed loco that stopped the broken con-rod from falling to the ground. *Author*

station, as this was not a regular stop. Both men climbed up onto the footplate to ask the driver what was wrong.

The driver told his story before fainting from sheer stress, with the worry of the passengers, knocking his head as he fell. The Station Master rang for an ambulance at once from his office. The driver said that he had heard a loud bang from the front left-hand side near the piston, and next thing steam was gushing from the cylinder. He slowed the locomotive down at once. The fireman leaned out of the cab window and saw that the con-rod had broken – it had come away from the crosshead but was still in the slide bars and had not dropped. Had it dropped to the ground, the 'Castle' would have turned over on its side, causing a major derailment. The piston rod was still connected to the crosshead, but the cylinder cover was gone, broken away from the studs and nuts, and the piston was hanging out of the cylinder. The piston cover was never found. When the con-rod had come back into the next revolution it had pushed the crosshead forward into the piston gland, the force as the piston flew against the cover causing it to blow out onto the line; it was made of cast iron and was very heavy.

Paul arranged with the Station Master to ring the signalman at East signal box and to move the station pilot on standby into position. While this was happening a spare driver came up from the shed to replace the original one. The 'Castle' was slowly taken off the main line and Jimmy, the workshop Fitter, met it at the entrance line into the shed and walked back beside it, making sure nothing fell off. Paul and Bob rode on the footplate. The locomotive was taken to the ash pan area near the coal stage to have the fire removed. Everybody went to the coal stage to have a look at what had happened, and No 1 road was made ready to receive the 'Castle' into the Lifting Shop. Meanwhile the station standby loco was pulling the passenger train out of the station towards London with a main-line crew aboard.

The locomotive was shunted into the Lifting Shop, the shunting loco was uncoupled and went out, and the main double doors were closed to keep the building warm. Then work started on making notes and ordering parts. Someone would have to go to Swindon with the list; for all main sheds that had their own workshops on the Great Western Railway, it was quicker for an apprentice to travel to Swindon than to put the order in the internal mailbag. Everything was replaced with new, and all the items came into the Fitting Shop in a covered wagon from Swindon: con-rod, crosshead, piston and rings, cylinder cover, and new studs with nuts. The large items were lifted out on the hoist using block and tackle and placed on the floor to be checked off against the work sheet.

The ring of studs were refitted into the cylinder head, after taking out the old and bent ones, and the set of piston rings were fitted into the cylinder. Their sizes were marked off, then they went into a vice on the work bench on the same mark and were knocked with a 2lb hammer; they were very brittle, and very sharp. We then fitted the rings into the groove in the piston with some graphite paste. Two of us lifted the piston manually and pushed it into the cylinder until the rings stopped us; two thin, flat metal bars were then used for edging the rings against the piston so that they would slide into the cylinder, Jimmy hitting the piston head with a soft white-metal hammer, which had been made on the forge from white-metal ingots. Then with a big rush of air in went the piston, and you looked down at your hands to see if your fingers were still there. Everything was lifted by hand or held up on crowbars jammed into the spokes of the driving wheels.

But the best was yet to come. The cylinder cover must have weighed a couple of hundredweight, as well as being under the running-plate of the locomotive. After smearing the cylinder face with graphite paste around the studs, two men and one boy – me – lifted the cover onto wooden blocks with the help of two crowbars, then, balancing the cover, it went straight up into the air, being pushed at the same time to reach the studs. A nut was quickly fitted onto a stud projecting from its little hole, leaving us sweating like pigs and wiping the sweat away with cotton waste. The piston was then connected to the crosshead, then the con-rod, the other end of which was then fitted to the driving wheel. We re-packed the gland with new graphite packing cut to size and tightened the gland down. At the end of March No 7008 *Swansea Castle* left Didcot.

●

These were good times. Bengy and I started to mate up at nights, meeting at the Labour Club for a drink and then across to the Railway Staff Club. Bill was a Fitter's mate, and also the Labour Club Steward in the evenings. He used to go for us and tell everyone we were underage, but he was a good sort, and we crossed his palm with silver, bought him a

Lamb's Navy rum and asked him nicely to keep quiet. That was all he drank, being an old Navy man, and all he smoked were Woodbines. Thursday nights was the best time to go out. We would go upstairs to the AEEU (Amalgamated Engineering & Electrical Union) meetings – we were all brothers. All the other Fitters also used to come down to the meetings; they would buy Bengy and me drink and we would go home merry. It was a free night – we were not allowed to pay. They were some good lads, but they tried to steer us.

Somehow the railway found out that I had been a schoolboy swimming champion in 1959, and they wrote to me to ask if I would swim for them at Blackpool. 'Yes,' was my reply. (I had also been Captain for the Corinthian team at St Birinus School in 1959, and it had been a great honour receiving the trophy in front of the whole school.) My Dad was delighted. We were sent our free passes and travel arrangements and were ready to go when we were notified that the event had been cancelled. I was bitterly disappointed.

So we went into the cabin, or mess room. The door was made of oak with a huge handle, and in the middle of the cabin was a pot-belly-type stove with an ash pan at the base. I took off the lid, stoked up the fire with coal, and took out the draught plate at the bottom. Someone asked what I was doing. I said that I was cold, although it was spring. Bengy shut the window and locked it. By this time the belly on the stove was glowing red-hot, so I dropped the draught plate back down. Then I opened the top plate with the handle. Everyone was reading papers and talking to one another, so they didn't see me drop four .22 bullets into the stove. Bengy and I walked out quickly but quietly, then all we could hear was someone shouting. We both got a hell of a telling-off from Arthur Brinkley, the Foreman. It had cleared the soot from the stack pipe, but all over the floor, and we had to clear it up. Poor old Bob, it shook him to bits! But the Fitters got their own back several times over the years.

On Fridays we didn't go home to dinner but cycled over to the hostel and bought fish and chips, bread and butter and a mug of tea for about a shilling. The food was good and there was plenty of it. Sometimes I would go on the station to the café and have a cup of tea just to see different people and watch the locomotives coming in.

Bengy and I were swapped around a lot with different Fitters. I would go with Fitter Ted Powell, who lived at the bottom of Station Road in the railway houses, while Frank Dowding, who lived up the top end of Kynaston Road, was Ted's mate. Their job was the inspection of locomotives when they came in and had their fire and ashes dropped at the ash pan area by the coal shed. With the fire gone there was still enough steam to do their tests, then the shed driver or fireman would bring the locomotive into the shed. Sometimes I would ride on the locomotive or, if no one was about, the driver would sometimes allow me to drive it down to the turntable. There we would balance it on the table, put on the vacuum brake, wind on the tender brake, climb down and push the table round to leave the smokebox door pointing towards London. We would then lock the table, get up onto the locomotive again and wind off the tender brakes, taking care when removing the chain that the handle did not spring back and hit us. Then we wound into forward gear, released the vacuum brake, opened up the regulator and away we would go. Then the driver would shunt into the shed.

Mick Gleason was the shed firelighter, who lit up the locomotives ready for duty; this would take up to 6 hours or more. He collected wooden sticks nailed into blocks and put them onto his shovel; a fireman's shovel was long with its sides folded upwards. In the middle of the sticks he would place cotton waste, and soak the lot in paraffin. Then he would light the cotton waste and place the package in the firebox, then pack coal around the burning waste with a few small lumps around and over the waste. He would check the fire every half-hour till it caught the coal, then he would shut the firebox doors and the smoke would gently rise out of the chimney and stink the whole place out. Mick would check the fire every hour after that, filling the firebox regularly with coal at the sides and front, then the steam gauge would start to rise till the fireman came in to take over some 45

minutes before the locomotive was required to leave the shed.

Sometimes the firelighter brought a shovel of burning coal from another locomotive to start the fire and occasionally a nasty accident occurred when a shed cleaner or an apprentice Fitter was in the firebox keeping out of the way of the Chargehand.

In May 1961 my Dad got his transfer to the shed as a Boiler Cleaner with Trevor May. It was a dirty job those two had. They were soaked to the skin and covered in grease. Their job was taking out the mud hole doors under the locomotive and along the sides of the boiler, then, using a water and steam hose connected up to the boiler, they would blow out the scale and sludge into the pit. The idea was to clear the boiler of hardened water and the build-up of muck in the tubes, which came out in lumps of white scale. The mud hole door was a cast-iron oval plate with a three-quarter-inch threaded screw protruding from the middle, onto which was fitted a bar with a hole in the middle. The idea was to insert the plate with a one-size graphite joint into the boiler on its side by holding the threaded screw. Firmly tightening a nut on the thread with a 2-foot-long spanner bar would clamp the bar to the face of the boiler.

Trevor and Dad had about five locomotives a day to do, and would shout instructions to each other. God help anyone who got in their way – they would turn the water hoses on them. My Dad was a villain; I think that's why I'm like him. Once I was pulled aside with his big hand across my ear, and he asked if I was selling 'French letters' (condoms) on the side. I was, but I didn't tell him. I lied to my Father that day, although we were a Catholic family.

When I was working with Fitter Jim Holmer we had to remove a safety valve from a '73xx' 2-6-0 locomotive because the gasket joint had blown. First we removed the outer casing, then we removed all the nuts around the safety valve. We lifted off the valve then, crouching down with the weight, one of us walked backwards with the other following onto the flat cab roof. There Jim scraped off the joint while I worked on the casting where the valve sat on top of the boiler.

I was using a chisel to scrape off the old

Fitter Jim Holmer stands on the left of this group of Didcot shed staff. Next to him is Reg Warr (Shed Foreman), Jim Tyler (Fitter), Cyril Dawson (Boilersmith), not known, Matt Oglesby (Fitter's mate), Burt Passey (Fitter), Bob Looms (Fitter), and another not known. Bengy is on the side steps and I am on the footplate. The locomotive is 'Hall' 4-6-0 No 6952 *Kimberley Hall*, which has just come out of the Lifting Shop after Jimmy and I had worked on it.

There are many old buildings around the country where the guidebooks say 'Queen Elizabeth I slept here', but the vast majority are believed to be untrue. During her reign (1558-1603) Kimberley Hall at Wymondham in Norfolk, owned by the Wodehouse family, occasionally acted as host to Good Queen Bess when she toured the country in her state coach holding court in the many places she visited. The family had a Royal throne built in the house for the Queen's use. The old house was pulled down in 1659 and a new one built on the same site, incorporating the historic Royal throne, which is still there to this day.

No 6952 was built at Swindon in February 1943, but the nameplate was not fitted until 29 September 1948 due to the shortage of brass during and after the Second World War. She cost £5,600 for the locomotive and boiler, and £1,408 for the Collett 4,000-gallon tender. She went first to Didcot on 23 February 1943 before moving around the Western Region. She returned in August 1950 and again in March 1959, after having three rows of superheaters fitted to her boiler. She moved on to Banbury in May 1965, and her last shed was Tyseley, from where she was withdrawn from service and, like so many locomotives, went to the scrapyards at Cashmore's at Great Bridge, having achieved a total mileage of 686,211. (The highest mileage for any GWR locomotive was the 2,429,722 of No 4037 *Queen Philippa*). *Author's collection*

joint, but it slipped out of my hand and fell between the boiler tubes. I was as sick as a pig – I had only made it on the forge the week before. We scraped both valve faces, refitted the valve and fitted the casing back on, pulling all the nuts down tight with a spanner and an iron tube, one of us pushing down on the spanner and the other pulling the tube with one hand gripping the handrail (in case we slipped off the side frame and fell down

onto the floor, about 6-7 feet below). Six months later Trevor and Dad washed out the scale from the boiler and I was called into the shed to be presented with my chisel! It had dropped down through the tubes and out through a mud hole door, under the locomotive. I still have it today in my toolbox.

An old stationary boiler was used to keep the steam and hot water flowing for Didcot shed. It comprised the boilers from two Pannier tanks,

No 4959 *Purley Hall* on No 2 road in Didcot Shed. Note the standpipes on the right for steam-cleaning the boilers. *Author*

The loco has passed through the shed on No 3 road, with the Lifting Shop in the background. The tall chimney is for the stationary shed boiler. *Author*

Nos 1509 and 1766, and was stationed next to the Fitting Shop and No 3 road. The shed staff kept an eye on the fire to keep it going all the time. Many times the coal would get low, then a shed 'tanky' would bring in a wagon full to be shovelled off into the bunker with help from the cleaners. In cold weather the boiler would never be allowed to go cold, it was too important. My Dad and Trevor also cleaned out this boiler on a quarterly routine.

Dad had transferred because he had day shifts, five days a week, and a Saturday morning. Later on he left the railway and went to Morris Motors in Cowley, Oxford, driving cars off the assembly line. He also ran a boxing club for the young at Didcot in the old hostels near the football ground in Station Road. He was trainer and referee and judge all rolled into one, and was well thought of. He was a lightweight boxer himself and had won the Leinster Championships; he was also a member of the Arbour Hill Boxing Club in Dublin. He boxed for the Army and was selected to box for Ireland in the Golden Gloves Championships in America after the Second World War.

One day he had a warm-up fight in Glasgow and his opponent rabbit-punched him on the back of his neck and broke it, but luckily not his spinal cord. He had to lay on his stomach for two years in a hospital ward. His fingertips had no feeling in them. He was discharged from the Royal Army Ordinance Corps after joining up, like many other Irish men, to fight against Hitler.

●

On 12 May the breakdown van was called out again. Bengy went with it but I had to stay in the shed. A coal truck had been shunted off the road in Didcot marshalling yard; Bengy said it had jumped the points.

The shed locomotive was a '61xx' 2-6-2T with the front end connected to the breakdown van and guard's van. Brink and his men stayed in the van while Bengy made the tea. Meanwhile I had to work with Dave back at the shed, stripping out the pistons of the inside cylinders of a '37xx' 0-6-0T, then packing them. There wasn't much room to move and there was no way pistons could be packed from the pit. The only way to do it – because I was thin – was to throw a sack across the con-rods and climb in under the boiler sideways, or sometimes I used to go in feet first on my back with a flare lamp for illumination. I would then sit across the con-rods with my feet dangling and a sack to stop the cold getting to my bum! I could then pull out the glands on the pistons after undoing the nuts, and also the packing. Dave cut the new packing to size and handed

the nuts and packing back to me. I fitted them back up into the piston porthole. When I had tightened the nuts I would climb out dirty and covered in grime.

On Thursday 16 June Bengy and I reported at work and went into the cabin. The place was empty. There was no one about, and it was the same in the Lifting Shop. We both got the forge lit up in case we had to smelt ingots to make castings. I went outside and the breakdown van was gone. Ted and Frank were the only two left on the shed and they told us to go with them until Brink and the lads came back. They said that a locomotive had jumped the rails at Foxhall and both cranes were out, one from Swindon and the other from Old Oak Common. The locomotive was No 7912 *Little Linford Hall*, and was 'off the road all wheels'. It was working a parcels train towards Birmingham and had hit a set of catch points at Foxhall signal box and jumped the line. Luckily no one had been hurt. The Didcot lads had been out all night, and someone had been sent to get hot food for them.

Bengy and I stayed in the shed just helping out, as we were short-staffed. We could see the cranes working from the station and could hear the noise, the cranes banging when the safety catches hit the wire drums in case something slipped. These cranes were operated by steam; they had their own boilers and were very powerful pieces of equipment.

The main line was closed both ways so the traffic was re-routed back as far as Reading. The Oxford line wasn't affected, so trains ran normally to there, but Swindon and Bristol

Pannier tank No 8743 is seen at Old Oak Common in February 1964. To get to the inside cylinders of these engines I would slide in through the gap beneath the water tank near the toolbox and wheel guard above the step. *Derek Everson*

trains could not get through. They eventually lifted the locomotive back on the road, and the breakdown van came back in as Bengy and I were going home at 5.00pm. The lads gave us some lip and we retaliated, all in good fun. We found out next day that they had been 'knocked up' in the night by a shedman who had gone out on his pushbike with all the emergency men's addresses. They said they were shattered after having worked all night, and came in the next day in dribs and drabs, whenever they had had enough sleep. Then, after the area had been cleared, in went the permanent way gang to put the road back together, fit new sleepers and rails and repack the ballast under the sleepers to get the main line open again.

Right No 4972 *St Brides Hall* runs on to the west curve to Oxford at Foxhall Junction signal box, Didcot, with the Weymouth parcels. It was a derailed 'Hall' that blocked the main line at Foxhall in June 1961. *R. J. Russell*

Below A 1964 view looking west towards Swindon from Foxhall bridge. Foxhall Junction signal box is in the right distance, with the GWR main line on the left. *R. J. Russell*

Left Looking east back towards Foxhall Bridge and Didcot station, Foxhall Junction signal box can be seen beyond the splitting Home signals for the West Curve. The small signal arm was for shunting. *R. J. Russell*

Above The same signal is seen in this view from the signal box, showing the crossovers from the main lines to the relief lines and West Curve. *R. J. Russell*

Below Inside Foxhall Junction signal box: G. Hopkinson is sitting, and M. Russell is standing at the frame. The door behind the stove was the toilet; this was such a busy box that there was never time to go to a toilet downstairs, where they were located in most boxes. *R. J. Russell*

Left The locking room beneath the operating floor of Foxhall Junction signal box, showing the complicated interlocking system. *R. J. Russell*

Above The West Curve at Foxhall Junction, leading to the Oxford line, was and still is on a very tight curve, and embedded in the ballast between sleepers outside the signal box was a self-greasing device called The Mills Hurcol Lubricator. It was filled with grease quarterly by maintenance, and the idea was that as a locomotive's flanged wheel drove round the tight curve the mechanical lever was pushed down and the grease was squeezed onto the inner surface of the rail to lubricate the side of the flange. The noise from metal flanges squealing on a railway line was unbearable, especially with short-wheelbase wagons that had fixed axles with no side play. Also, if wheel flanges were not checked regularly there was a danger that a train might fall off the road. *R. J. Russell*

Train runs into derailed wagons

Derailed wagons on the railway near Didcot today.

DIDCOT CRASH DELAYS SERVICES

AFTER eight wagons and trucks of a goods train had been derailed a quarter of a mile west of Didcot station early to-day, a second goods train ran into the trucks.

Eight wagons of an Ipswich to Cardiff train and one of a Reading-Cardiff train were derailed.

Left A newspaper cutting from Wednesday 28 June, showing Arthur Brinkley, our Workshop Foreman, and to the right of him Jimmy Tyler, at Foxhall Junction signal box. *Author's collection*

Just 13 days later another crash happened at Foxhall. I remember it was early morning, and when we came to work the breakdown van was out. So Bengy and I asked the Shed Foreman if we might leave the shed, and we went off to Foxhall signal box to see what was going on. Brink said it was OK for us to be there and we helped clear up the mess and made tea and coffee for the lads.

This time the main line was clear but the trains slowed down and people were looking at us clearing up the wreckage. What a mess, with box vans on their sides. It turned that out one train had run into the back of another. The signals and lines were ripped out of the ground so, when everything was cleared after the cranes were finished, the permanent way gang was back on the scene. The Swindon and Old Oak Common cranes were there again. After the crash was cleared we had a ride back in the breakdown van, then we had to clear it out ready for the next job – repack stores and provisions, wood and coal, and fill up the water tank on the roof.

On the subject of Foxhall, the GWR had a most beautiful pair of stained glass windows that came from the outbuildings of a very old farm that had to be demolished in 1884 when the Foxhall Curve was built over the land of Foxhall Farm at Didcot. The farm had originally been a Royal Hunting Box built for King James II of England (1685-88), who was also James VII of Scotland. The design in each diamond of the windows was the Tudor Rose of England or the Thistle of Scotland, which gives us a clue that the windows were installed before 1801, as the Act of the Union with Ireland was passed in that year. The glass is of a dark bottle-green hue, which has not been manufactured for at least 200 years, and would have been made by hand.

One day during the early 20th century a fox was being pursued by hounds at Didcot and was watched from the window of a railway carriage. The fox approached the moving train and suddenly leapt through the window, which was open, and crawled under the seat. The hounds soon lost the scent and were left behind. Some miles further on the fox suddenly jumped out through the window again and sped across the countryside, out of sight.

Foxhunts were common between the wars and every Great Western Railway driver who was worth his title knew exactly how to deal with the problem when he saw a pack of hounds chasing a fox that looked as if it might be crossing the line. Foxes liked trains and knew how to get across the line and leave the dogs unable to follow them. A driver would invariably get very close to the hounds then suddenly use all his skills to stop the train just in the nick of time before running over the dogs. The grateful Master of Foxhounds would ride up alongside the stopped locomotive and hand the driver a golden sovereign (three days' pay), with half a sovereign for his fireman. Little did the generous huntsman know that the crafty driver had carefully adjusted his speed a long way back to engineer the situation. He would have found himself with a very aggrieved fireman had he let the hounds cross the line behind the train.

●

It was the great day for my old mate Bengy when, on 29 June 1961, he went off to sign his five-year apprenticeship papers. He didn't go to London like me but signed in the Shedmaster's office – I think the word was 'pleased'!

In the afternoons, if there was not much work, Bengy and I would go across to the carriage sidings, where there would be a gang of blokes shouting among themselves. Right in the middle was Dai Davis (who eventually became my brother Dick's father-in-law); he had a flat piece of wood with two old pennies on, and he would then flip the end up in the air and the coins would come down odds or evens. I have never seen so much money betted on a game, including £1 notes, the old green ones.

I also got to know Mick Howard and we went everywhere together. His Mum used to invite me around for tea on Saturdays. Mick lived in the same road as me and after tea we would go to the White Hart on The Broadway or stay at his house, push the sofa to the wall, put on records and jive with his sister Jenny, while Mick's Mum would clap and join in. What lovely times we had!

Mick worked in the Parcels Depot, near the Provender Stores. He was also mated out with a chap called Pete Brown as a second man delivering parcels to houses and businesses. The Parcels Depot had a contract to move some bales of Irish peat from Upton station to the Johnson Houghton horse-racing stables at Blewbury on the Downs. In the sidings at Upton there would be two box vans full of peat; Pete drove a lorry, so we would load and deliver all day long for maybe two Saturdays. I think we earned a few bob. What was left in the bottom of the lorry I used to bag up, take home and sell at 2s 6d per sackful to people who grew roses.

Mick and I used to go out on Thursday nights after we got paid – I now had £2 10s, having completed a year's service. The hours dropped to 44 per week, so we lost 4 hours but got paid the same. My Mum had £1 17s 6d for housekeeping, which left me 12s 6d a week. Beer was 1s 6d a pint for a brown and mild (nicknamed 'boilers'), which was all we drank, plus a shot of Lamb's Navy rum, neat, at half a crown (2s 6d).

We also used to go out dancing at the Oxford Ballrooms at Reading on Saturday nights. Thus we were broke by Sunday. But all the firemen were there, and girls; we would meet at Didcot Post Office and catch O'Brien's coach, which laid on the transport there and back for a small fee. This went on for a few years every Saturday. I was never asked my age for drinking.

●

One Monday morning in September Bengy and I had to report to Brinkley, who had been asked to get us booked in for night school twice a week. I went to Engineering Drawing on Mondays and Science and Maths on Wednesdays. I had to bring proof to Brink to say which courses I was doing, and Bengy did the same.

Sometimes we had rotten jobs to do. One was to put on a helmet with a lamp attached and batteries on your belt, climb into the pit at the ash pan dump and go underneath looking for a body or bits of one when a locomotive had run over a person. Once I only

Mick Howard with my Mum in 1961. *Author*

found a pair of boots caught in the damper under the firebox. I think you can guess the rest.

As the apprentices were the thinnest of all the crews, another job, when the Fitters had drained the tender of water, was to climb into the filling hole and drop into the inner tank, where the water was up to your knees. We would then climb through the webbing looking for any body parts that, it was supposed, may have been scooped up into the tender. All I found were eels and snakes and a few dead birds. While I was in the empty tender the Fitters and their mates would hammer on the side, to get their own back on us.

On the Pannier tanks, if the water-level float in the cab didn't work correctly the Fitter would drain the side tanks then we apprentices would drop into the filler hole with our arms up in the air. We would then wriggle through the webbing to the float gauge and connect up the ball-float lever, which had

Didcot's locomotive allocation in October 1961

0-6-0	2-6-0	2-6-2T	2-8-0	4-6-0 'Hall'
2221	5380[2]	6109	2836	4902 *Aldenham Hall*
2230	6302	6120	2849	4910 *Blaisdon Hall*
	6313	6124[3]	2893	4915 *Condover Hall*
0-6-0PT	6350	6130	2898	4939 *Littleton Hall*
3665[1]	6363	6136	3819	4950 *Patshull Hall*
3751	7324	6139	3820	4959 *Purley Hall*
5746 (NBL)	7327	6159	3840	4965 *Rood Ashton Hall*
8494 (RSH)				4969 *Shugborough Hall*
8720 (BP)				4976 *Warfield Hall*[4]
9450 (RSH)		**4-6-0 'County'**		5987 *Brocket Hall*
		1002 *County of Berks*		6910 *Gossington Hall*
		1007 *County of Brecknock*		6937 *Conyngham Hall*
		1015 *County of Gloucester*		
		1018 *County of Leicester*		**4-6-0 'Modified Hall'**

All were Swindon-built except those marked NBL (North British Locomotive Co Ltd), BP (Beyer Peacock Co Ltd) and RSH (Robert Stephenson & Hawthorns Ltd)

6969 *Wraysbury Hall*
6983 *Otterington Hall*
6996 *Blackwell Hall*

[1] No 3665 arrived on 24 October 1961
[2] No 5380 arrived on 26 October 1961
[3] No 6124 arrived from Slough on 24 October 1961
[4] No 4976 left for Swindon on 4 October 1961
No 6145 stayed at Didcot until 19 October 1961

Below A young engine cleaner working on No 6969 *Wraysbury Hall*, one of Didcot's allocation, on No 2 road. *Author*

Below Another Didcot 'Hall', No 6937 *Conyngham Hall*, on No 3 road. *Author*

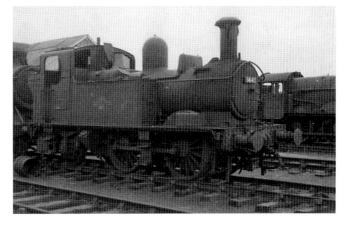

Above Less lucky were these engines at Didcot awaiting scrapping in 1960/61, with 0-4-2T No 1445 on the right. Many still had years of life left in them. *R. J. Russell*

Right A closer view of No 1445, ready to be scrapped. Note that the chimney has sacking tied over it. *R. J. Russell*

Right 2-8-0 No 4707 at Didcot shed, also waiting to be scrapped, some time in the mid-1960s. *R. J. Russell*

come undone. These were difficult tanks because the way you went in was the way you came out, with no other way to move but to lie on your side. Again, the Fitters would hammer on the side to frighten us. The truth was that they couldn't fit into a small tank hole, whereas we could.

In November Bonfire Night came round, and Bengy and I were fooling about on the waste ground behind the breakdown van. We both had a pocket full of penny bangers bought from the local paper shop in Station Road, and were lighting them and throwing them at each other, jumping aside as they exploded, or hiding behind a coach as one went off by our feet. Being clever, I found a small empty whisky bottle in an old dustbin, lit a banger and dropped it in. I do not know to this day why I hung around, screwing the cap back on the bottle – yes, it blew up in my face, catching both of my eyes and blinding me for 30-40 minutes. My eyes were bloodshot, and I fell to the ground, holding my face and eyes. The glass from the bottle also cut across my eyes. I was very lucky I was

not blinded, and it taught me a lesson not to play with fireworks, especially bangers, again.

Christmas was upon us once again, so Bengy and I went into the cabin to sing the Christmas carols as we had last year. The cabin door was left open and the rest of the shed staff were there, including Boilersmiths Cyril Dawson, Frank Marshall, Johnny Cooper, old Jack Dearlove, Boilerwashers Trevor May and Chris Kelly, some drivers and firemen, Jim Parson, the Storeman, all the Fitters and their mates who were on days, and of course Brink. Bengy and I started off and everyone joined in. What a good way to start Christmas! As usual the Fitters and their mates put their hands in their pockets. Bengy always said that I sang like a bird, because I got paid for doing it and wouldn't stop!

That Christmas Eve I went around to my mate Mick's house, where his Mum was packing up a basket of food and a few bottles of beer. Mick and I went down to the hostel by the Staff Club looking for a chap that Mick worked with in the Parcels Depot; like many others, Tom lived away from his home all year

Braziers burning in the shed on a cold frosty morning. Author

round. It was heartbreaking: a bed, a small side table and a few photos. Mick wished him a happy Christmas, and Tom broke down in tears as he opened the food. He asked us to stay and have a drink, so we had a bottle of beer with him, wished him a happy Christmas, then pulled out a half-bottle of whisky for him; Mick and I went halves with the cost. We both ended up in the Labour Club across the road and then went into the Railway Club. Then we staggered home, having done our good turn for the day.

We arrived back at work after Boxing Day to find the shed deep in snow. It was the start of a bad winter to come. It snowed heavily all day and for many days after that, and both night and day it was very cold. The locomotives froze up, and all the shed staff, including the drivers, Fitters and mates froze up as well. Bengy and I kept the braziers ('fire devils') filled up with coal, and stood them as near as possible to the locomotives. The braziers were shaped like huge rounded metal basket grates and stood on iron legs. All the Fitters and their mates carried iron rods with cotton waste tied to them; these were dipped in paraffin and ignited to melt the ice under the cylinder steam cocks. They also freed off the water pipes connecting the tender to the locomotive. The tracks were covered in snow, and sometimes the only thing you could see was just two black lines running along – no sleepers at all.

We heard Brink shout to get over to the east loop line quickly. A train had stopped at a signal and had started to freeze up. So there was Jim Tyler, Jim Holmer, Dave Davis, Bengy and me surrounded by the fumes from burning waste. Suddenly there was a roar and a bang from the steam cocks – the driver had the signal clear and away he went with the 'Grange' 4-6-0 and a load of bananas on his tail. As he headed off he blew his whistle and both the crew waved, then pulled the cab sheet back into place to stop the cold getting to them. We returned to the shed to keep on freeing off locomotives and topping up the braziers with coal, as well making sure that all the sandboxes were free for the sand to flow if needed to stop the locomotives' wheels from slipping.

In the shed most of the locomotives were fired up and the fireboxes were full and very hot. I would climb up onto the footplate with half a loaf of bread and a toasting fork and open up the firehole doors to make toast. I would then climb down into the cabin, slap on the butter and cheese, and enjoy a mug of tea – lovely!

On 29 December I noticed that the air starting to feel different, as it had about the same time the previous year, when it turned cold and foggy. Then a freak storm blew up the wind and snow came again, as on Boxing Day. There was -22 degrees of frost and the points froze up again and again. There was so much snow about on the roads that it was shovelled up and put into tipper lorries, then dumped in the River Thames to get rid of it. Men continuously burned cotton waste and paraffin on the point rodding from the signal boxes; they were totally exhausted with the cold and snow and the pressure of work to get the trains through.

3
1962: SHED LIFE

Surprisingly, perhaps, the heaviest snowfall around the Didcot district had occurred on 25 April 1908. The snow fell from the Midlands to the Isle of Wight, but the biggest fall was around Didcot, and gave the Great Western Railway its biggest headache, with train services from Portsmouth, Southampton, Bristol, South Wales, Bournemouth and Birkenhead delayed. With high winds blowing the snow across the points, jamming them and preventing movement, and the signals the same, it was nearly impossible to get anywhere.

Didcot had more than 140 sets of points around the junction, so everything started to slow down with the snow getting worse. Trains managed to run on the main line from Reading to Didcot, but the lines to Oxford and the north and the Berks & Hants line from Reading were blocked, and all movement came to a stop. From Didcot to Newbury the lines were blocked for more than 5 hours and could not be used till the snowploughs were called out to clear the line to Winchester. The snowploughs would only work on the single-line routes from Didcot, which were kept open by the efforts of GWR railwaymen and dedicated staff.

Things got so bad that the Signal Engineer at Reading and the Locomotive Department at Swindon organised special gangs of railwaymen to work between their areas to keep the main lines open. With the weather getting worse, telegraph wires were brought down by the weight of snow between Reading and Tilehurst and on to Goring in Berkshire. Meanwhile a locomotive came off the road at the crossover points on the Berks & Hants line at Reading, blocking the two lines for more than 3 hours, during which there was no movement. The single-line Electric Train Staff apparatus failed between Wheatley and Littlemore in Oxfordshire, and there was another derailment in Paddington marshalling yard.

Snow storms were intermittent during the following night, then snow fell over Slough with extreme force, but did not lay at any depth. Only east of Reading did any working difficulties appear, with some express trains diverted via Maidenhead and Wycombe to Oxford.

That April day in 1908 was also the date of the football Final being played at Crystal Palace, and 23 return excursion trains were worked from Paddington. Despite serious 3-hour delays for trains working through Didcot, they all got to the football match on time without mishap. Through trains from and to London were badly delayed, some for more than 4 hours. Special trains started out from Swindon, Bristol and other stations to the West of England and South Wales to maintain the more important services, and some had to be stopped to pick up and set down delayed passengers at different stations.

At Paddington more than 100 passengers finally arrived by trains after 1.00am. They remained in the waiting rooms or in a train at the platform with warm steam-heated coaches for their comfort. Other passengers who could not reach their stations left their trains and went to hotels for the night. The steam heating on the trains greatly minimised the inconvenience to passengers, and very few people complained.

Goods trains that had been suspended on 25 April went back into operation in the early hours of the Sunday morning.

Meanwhile, on 3 January 1962 we were also experiencing a blizzard as snow fell over Berkshire. On the 5th there was a severe frost, -15 degrees. It had been very cold since Boxing Day and the radio said it was the worst on record since 1939. Sixteen inches of snow fell at Didcot and the weather was getting much colder, going down to -30 degrees of frost.

We used to go across to the ash pan area with a bucket to collect red-hot ashes so that we could put the tools in to warm them up; otherwise the skin would tear away from your hands, they were so cold. We were still trying to free the locomotives from ice, and were burning waste around the steam cocks under the pistons. We also climbed between tender and locomotive to free off the water pipes.

At the bottom of No 8 road there was a stockpiled heap of coal; the coal stage was not being used as the coal wagons couldn't get up the slope. With snow on top the heap looked like the Alps, so we took dustbin lids, climbed to the top and slid down until we got fed up and cold and wet. There was also an empty coal wagon there, so we pushed it up towards the shed and applied the brake. We then put some detonators on the line, went back, let off the brake, pushed the wagon and jumped on. Bang! Bang! Bang! Everyone came running out of the Lifting Shop at the sound of the explosions.

We had also put some detonators into a barrel that was burning by the coal heap, and let them blow up. It blew the barrel to pieces. A trackman was walking past, checking the keys (wooden blocks) in the rails and the fishplates. He saw us and we had a telling-off from Jimmy, who reported us to Brink!

Bengy and I clocked off one night at 5.00pm and had to walk home; in the snow there was no way we could ride a bike. In those days there was no salt or grit put down, and people struggled with great effort to get about. We were walking across to the ash pan area over the bottom of the hump when, with a mighty crash, we saw a hydrant explode into the air and water gush out. Someone ran to isolate it and the water around just froze. We both legged it home. (They used the hydrants for washing down the ashes.)

During 1962 ex-GWR 4-6-0 No 6000 *King George V* came into the shed, one of 30 of these very strong and quite spectacular locomotives. Cor! What a sight! She was so lovely, and it seemed that she was always freshly painted and all the visible brass parts were shining – 'King of the road'! With her great driving wheels and con-rods and the Great Western green livery, in my opinion she was the best. I was so proud to see her and climb up on the front end by the smokebox and touch the famous bell, which was a gift from the centenary celebrations of the Baltimore & Ohio Railroad in October 1927 – it is something I will never forget. She had to have a bell fitted, as that was the practice in the United States. The bell was never removed after her visit, and today she is preserved. I never saw her at Didcot after that; she was an Old Oak Common (81A) engine. How I would have loved to have been the driver of *King George V*, even for only one day.

Pride was a quality much associated with the railways in their early days. In the 1890s the GWR introduced the 'Duke' Class 4-4-0s, and one of them was named *Comet*. She had the usual large dome on the boiler, which was shining brass, and her fireman would clean it every day. It looked very beautiful indeed, and on his rest day the driver would bring his family down to the shed with a picnic and sit next to the engine on the grass. The driver and fireman did odd jobs on the locomotive in their spare time, with the driver's son sitting across the boiler looking at himself in the brass dome; his distorted reflection was like a fairground hall of mirrors.

Until 1919 most drivers had their own permanent locomotives, and they liked to do all the minor repairs themselves, to avoid the locomotive being 'stopped' next day and a

The footplate of *King George V.* In the centre is the red-painted regulator handle The banjo-shape object above it is the vacuum brake, and above it the steam pressure gauge. On the right is the reversing gear, and above that the AWS (Automatic Warning System) equipment. At the bottom is the firebox, and on the left can be seen a boiler water level gauge. *Author*

spare locomotive being allocated to them for a few days. Then their working hours were reduced and long runs could no longer be done by one driver, so they could no longer have their own permanent locomotives.

Before the First World War the more important locomotives not only had their own footplate crew but the driver was also allowed to choose a cleaner from the shed staff to work solely on his locomotive, and that boy was allowed to select five other boys to work under him. Those boys were very proud young men to be allowed to be in charge of cleaning the locomotives. If they got into any misconduct they would be removed from the gang, with the associated disgrace.

Comet had standard arc nameplates, but her short five-letter name left blank spaces at both

ends. In 1937 at Didcot station a young fireman thought it very funny to add the letters 'IN' before the name and 'AX' after it: *INCOMETAX!*

A great many locomotives came into Didcot shed when I was serving my apprenticeship and I would climb up onto the footplate and admire them. These included members of the 'Castle' Class, built at Swindon from August 1923. The first was *Caerphilly Castle*, designed by C. B. Collett. With four cylinders, two rows of superheating and hydrostatic lubrication, they weighed less than 120 tons. Later they had bigger tenders, which brought the weight up to 126 tons 11 cwt. The last 'Castle' was built by BR in 1950 and was named *Swindon*. The 'Kings' took over from the 'Castles' in 1927 and were known as 'Super Castles'.

Spring came at last, and the weather was getting a bit better and warmer. Dave and Jim made a model boat propelled by some clockwork that Dave found at home. Dave was good at making models and tools, and was later to help me with making tools. They installed the clockwork in the hull and sealed the propeller, then balanced it with nuts for stability in the water trough next to the forge. They then sealed the whole of the boat, made a cabin and funnel and set the rudder. Water tests completed, Dave, Jim, Bengy and I walked to the reservoir by the Provender Stores, where the Great Western Railway once prepared food for its 4,000 horses. We had to cross over the roads at the back of the Lifting Shop, walk past the carriage sidings and over into the main centre yard; being a marshalling yard, we were looking out at all times for shunting locomotives and wagons. Then we crossed the main up and down lines between Didcot station and the Oxford line – in all, 14 roads.

This was it. The big day. The lake was huge and deep – no one ever found the bottom (in the 1950s two children had drowned in its 3,326,000 gallons of water). Dave wound up the motor and Jim set the rudder. I said they should have put a string on it in case they couldn't get it back, but I was told to keep my nose out. Off went the boat – the motion was wonderful and it glided through the water right out to the middle, and stopped! Dave looked at Jim, and Bengy and I nudged each other. I said, 'I told you so.' It sank in minutes, by the stern, just like a real ship. What a great sight! Bengy and I stood to attention, saluted and sang 'God Save the Queen'. Dave and Jim didn't think it very funny, but we couldn't stop laughing.

●

Then there was another breakdown – a few wagons were off in the centre marshalling yard, so out went the crew with the red-painted breakdown van and the black rest room van. It was a frosty morning and everything we touched was cold, but by mid-morning the sun was coming up. We got the wagons back on the road, and as I was helping with the jacks in the van I smelled bacon being cooked.

There was a locomotive – a 'Hall' Class 4-6-0 – stopped not far from us, so I climbed up to the footplate and the driver and fireman were having their breakfast. The fireman had a shiny clean shovel on which they were cooking their food. He placed his shovel just inside the firebox, with eggs and bacon sizzling away and a billycan of tea ready. What a lovely memory of long ago! That was how the footplate crews lived on these locomotives. Then I came back into the world and had to go back to the Lifting Shop.

The breakdown van was loaded and on its way back. A few of us walked across the roads back to the shed, looking left and right and listening for the sounds of moving trains. But the next moment a locomotive pulling a goods train passed within inches of us as we were about to cross over the next set of lines. Jim and Dave pulled me back against a box van and shouted to the others to look out – the loco's cylinder just missed all of us by inches. In a marshalling yard the lines were closer together and there was not much room to walk.

Mr Marriner, a shed labourer employed at Didcot in the 1950s, was not so lucky. He was 58 years old and had worked all his life at the same depot. One day he was asked to go across to the coal stage and clean out the pits, as they were filled with ash. This was a regular occurrence, as a locomotive would come into the shed to be coaled up, and the fireman would drop the fire or ash into the pit. On this occasion 2-8-0 No 2882 came into the coal stage to have its tender refilled and, having done so, the driver looked out of the side cab windows on both sides to make sure that no one was about. Seeing that the way was clear, he blew the whistle and opened the regulator slowly to move off. At that precise moment Mr Marriner decided to crawl out of the pit between the locomotive and tender. Who would do such a crazy thing? Bengy and I had, but we never got hurt, unlike this poor man. The locomotive ran over both his legs between the body and the knees, nearly severing them from his body.

The first aid man from the shed was sent for, and with an ordinary carpenter's saw he cut off both Mr Marriner's legs. He was then carried across to the main Oxford line where the shed staff had flagged down a passenger train. He was lifted up into the guard's van, which was the quickest way to get him to Oxford Hospital. His legs were placed with him. Mr Marriner died shortly after reaching hospital.

A worse accident had taken place on the GWR in 1870. A fireman was working with his driver, shunting and moving locomotives around the shed to be positioned for the next day's workings. The fireman, taking no notice of the driver and his warning, jumped off a moving locomotive as it was going through the ash pan area where the ashes were heaped high. He landed on the ashes and fell over, sliding down the ashes and under the moving locomotive. The poor man had his legs and arms amputated where the wheels ran over him. He died the next day. This was the only case of a man losing all four limbs in such circumstances.

●

Bengy and I made a catapult each – we bought the rubber from Mr Bosley's shop in Station Road – and went over to the sewage pits looking for duck eggs. Matt was with us one day. We had to walk between the pits on a

Above No 2879, a '28xx' Class 2-8-0, at Cardiff on 29 May 1962. She is a sister engine to the one featured in the accompanying sad story about the Didcot shed labourer. *Author's collection*

Left Water columns were used to fill locomotive tenders and tanks. The engine would pull alongside, then the driver would climb down off the footplate and get ready to turn on the water at the base of the column, while the fireman lifted the cover off the filler and pulled the canvas 'bag' into the hole. They were also useful for washing sewage off apprentices! This example is on the West Curve at Didcot. *R. J. Russell*

small path. You had to be careful, though – one slip and over into the sewage you would go.

Bengy shouted, 'Let's play commandos!' and jumped from one corner of the path to the other. You've guessed it – he hit the corner of the verge and went under. To say he smelled was an understatement. He stank to high heaven. We took him back to the loop line, keeping our distance from him. Matty and I were laughing all the way to the shed, and no doubt Bengy would have done the same had one of us fallen in the pit. We put him under the water column between Nos 1 and 2 roads

The '14xx' Class 0-4-2Ts were lovely-looking little engines and were used all over the former GWR lines on branch-line and push-and-pull work. No 1407 is leaving Wallingford station in 1953 *R. J. Russell/Author*

and turned on the water, which poured out from the canvas bag down on his head and all over his clothes. There was sewage everywhere. Matty and I got his clothes off and gave him a pair of overalls, and Brinkley sent him home. Bengy stank for days afterwards; he said he had had many baths and hair washes, but he still stank.

Mick Howard, Bengy and I started to mate up, and all three of us would go to Oxford on a Saturday evening, to the pictures then the pub. Sometimes we missed the last train home and caught the milk train, whose locomotive would likely be an old '63xx' Class 2-6-0, its big side rods clanking along the road to Didcot.

Then we seemed to lose Bengy. He met up with a girl named Marion in the pouring rain during the Didcot May Fair. Love at first sight! She was lovely – and they are still together today, living in Cornwall.

On a less pleasant note, I came into the shed one morning to find at the doorway of No 4 road a '14xx' Class 0-4-2T. She was covered in milk and blood and parts of cows, all over the leading end, buffers, smokebox, boiler and cab. Apparently she was coming home from Abingdon to Didcot and someone had left the gate open in a field. Twenty cows wandered onto the railway and the locomotive just ploughed through them. It was not a pleasant sight. The next time I saw the locomotive she had been cleaned down.

Meanwhile, the driver and fireman would have to put in their reports.

At that time at Didcot we had no one in the Lifting Shop who could braze or weld with gas bottles, so someone was sent to Reading or Oxford. One day I went to Oxford with a 10-15-foot vacuum pipe with a hole scored in it. The ends were tied up with sacking and string so that the dirt didn't get on my clothes. I also took a chitty with a number on it. I was given a workman's pass to go to Oxford, so waited for a suitable train. I chucked the labelled pipe into the guard's van and sat in the carriage. When I got off the train I collected the pipe and walked to the end of the platform and along the path to the shed. I found the Foreman, dropped the pipe in to the blacksmith and had a wander about. Dick, my brother, worked at Oxford, but he was on nights so I missed him. If these jobs took a while I would a walk about the town. I then returned to Didcot, where the Fitter, Paul Kelly, and his mate Bob Warrick were waiting to put it back under the locomotive and test it.

While waiting for the trains to travel to Reading or Oxford sheds, I would sit and watch the shunting in the main marshalling yard outside Didcot station, undertaken by a 'tanky' with a 'shunt dummy' – a truck in which all the shunting men's food and spare poles were kept. The shunters used to hang on to the hand rails or stand on the ledge while

A preserved 'shunt dummy', used to carry men and equipment around a shunting yard. *Author*

the locomotive was taking goods trains out and moving trucks about. They would stand ready to jump off and run down to uncouple a few wagons, then the locomotive would rush forward and suddenly stop, allowing the uncoupled trucks to travel on freely by themselves.

I would watch as the shunters ran down and stuck their poles into the brake levers, then jumped up onto the pole and sat there. As the wagons ran the shunter would drop the hand brake slowly to reduce the wagon's speed and prevent it from crashing into any others. He would then jump off the wagon and pull down the brake to stop it, then go underneath between the wagons and couple them to the rest of the goods train, with the guard's van at the end. The different wagons had different telegraphic code names: 'Toad', 'Crocodile', 'Mex', 'Serpent', 'Python', 'Loriot', 'Mogo' and 'Minx', to name but a few.

●

Bengy and I were off on our travels again, being moved around with different Fitters. I was moved to work with Jim Holmer, who lived in Didcot, while Bengy got moved to Paul, my brother. But if nothing was on, we met up and walked across the tracks to the Provender Stores, originally used for fodder for the railway horses; we found the best time to go was about 2 o'clock in the afternoon.

The Stores were built in 1885 and demolished after 91 years of service in 1976. Railway horses were once very important part of the Goods Department, and their manure also played a very important part at Swindon Works. When mixed with a special red sand from the GWR pit in Kidderminster, it made just the right substance for casting moulds, as used in the foundry. The Works at Swindon used several tons a week between the wars, and of course this valuable material originated from Didcot, because Didcot provided the hay that went into the Great Western's 4,000 horses that produced the manure.

Didcot Provender Stores in July 1962. Bengy and I climbed up on to the roof of the water tower to look over the countryside. *R. J. Russell*

In the Stores we found tea chests and crates, then we climbed the stairs to the next floor, from where we could see the old stables for the horses. The next floor was empty. Up again we went, through the skylight and out onto the roof, then across a plank to the water tower. There was no handrail, just a sheer drop. We climbed up the water tank steps onto the roof, where we had a view for miles – something I will never forget.

On the return trip to the shed we had to cross the up and down main lines again, then go into the centre marshalling yard. Bengy climbed over between wagons, where the coupling was, but I went underneath. All at once the train moved and, by God, I almost wet myself! I had to get out because the train was moving – and as the train moved along so did I, crawling along the sleepers, until I had the nerve to leap out into the open. It taught me a lesson – next time I would check if there was a locomotive on the end.

Later my father-in-law told me about the Second World War at Didcot, when a German aeroplane flew over the Ordnance Depot in November 1940. It was a Junkers 88 that had become separated from the main group, and as it flew over the pilot dropped two bombs, just missing the Ordnance Depot stores. He also strafed the store sheds with his machine guns but no one was hurt, although my future in-laws worked there at the time. As the Junkers 88 flew out over the Provender Stores he encountered a machine gun post situated on

A 1940 newspaper cutting showing the crashed German Junkers 88. *Author's collection*

top of the roof. The Army Sergeant in charge shot at the aeroplane without permission, but it flew away across the Home Counties until two Spitfires machine-gunned it. Then many people saw it on fire, and it eventually crashed on the Berkshire Downs near Blewbury.

My father-in-law was in the Home Guard in his spare time, and lived at Upton, 2 miles from Blewbury. He was duly put on guard duty next to the bomber. When I married his daughter I was given a small piece of the Junkers 88, which I still have today. The Army Sergeant was court-martialled for opening fire on the bomber without permission.

The Ordnance Depot was a main supply depot for the war, and many regiments worked in the area, as well as civilian personnel for the services. After the Depot closed in 1973 it was cleared to build the new Power Station. At that time I was working with a small company and we came upon one of the Depot's concrete sheds, which had the Ministry seal with the lock still attached to it. The company telephoned a few people to get the doors unlocked, and when they were slid back they revealed, still wrapped up in boxes, six Merlin Spitfire engines. They were later taken away.

Another wartime story involves 'Aberdare' Class 2-6-0 No 2652. Before the Normandy invasion the Americans wondered how long it would take to repair a steam locomotive after the RAF had shot it up, so they made arrangements with the Great Western Railway to borrow No 2652, which was near to being scrapped. The shed fireman was sent out to the local hardware shop to buy a few gallons of whitewash, then the locomotive was painted all over white so the Americans could recognise the target.

The engine was placed in position on a disused branch line, then the American aircraft attacked her as they would a train in France (although that one would be moving, while this one was standing still). The locomotive was then taken in a very battered condition to Newport Ebbw Junction Shed for repairs, and was put back into first-class condition. The Americans wanted to know just how many days the work would take, and they paid the whole cost.

●

One day I was working with Jimmy in the shed, on No 2 road at the entrance, as the whole line was blocked with locomotives. At the other end there were no buffers, only blocks on each rail. Working on the second locomotive in from the entrance, 'tanky' No 8720, I was up in the motions, in between the con-rods, packing pistons and valves, when there was a yell to clear the area. Coming in fast on No 2 road was a runaway.

Jimmy quickly pulled me down in the pit, out from the motions, and we both ran, partly crawling and keeping our heads and shoulders down, back towards the stop ends. We couldn't get out because all the locomotives were buffer to buffer, so we stayed in the pit where we were, under the tender of the last loco. In came the runaway, hit the first locomotive and crashed and shunted every locomotive down to the last onto the blocks. We were frightened but unhurt. The locomotive we were working on had to have the buffer replaced, as it broke off. This was a two-man job, using the cradle rail trolley.

The story was that a young fireman was shunting 'dead' locomotives into the shed (meaning that they had no steam), then driving out to shunt another one onto another road. When he reversed out of the shed, past the points, he shut the regulator and applied the vacuum brake to slow down the locomotive. He then pushed the gear lever into the forward position, slightly opened the regulator and climbed off the footplate. The locomotive drove on past the points until the gear change took effect. Meanwhile he pulled the points over, and as the locomotive came forward past him he climbed up the steps. But not this time – he slipped and fell off onto the ground. The runaway, a '61xx' Class 2-6-2T, duly came into the shed like the proverbial bat out of hell. When the fireman got up all he could do was shout 'Get clear!'

A similar thing had happened towards the end of 19th century, when a small tank engine left the locomotive shed at Slough, driven by the shed fireman. He was to take the 'tanky' up to the coaling stage to be refilled, while the driver went to the stores inside the shed for oil

and cotton waste, having instructed the fireman what to do. The fireman got off the footplate to pull the points over, but before doing so he opened the regulator; the 'tanky' began to move and pick up speed. Again, the young fireman thought he would have time to turn and get back onto the footplate and bring the engine into the coaling stage, but this operation was very dangerous. Before the young man could move the 'tanky' went by him at a speed of 15-20mph, and before he realised it was 400 yards up the road. He did try to chase the runaway but got nowhere. I imagine that by this time the young man had aged very quickly!

The engine demolished the stop blocks of one of the bay lines in the station and ran on through a brick wall, the wall being that of the District Engineer's office, although at the time he was not there. It went straight through the adjoining office wall, and the two clerks working inside both quickly jumped out through the windows. The 'tanky' eventually came to a standstill, having caused considerable damage to the station and the offices. But before stopping, a buffer had broken off its castings and flown through the platform fencing, hitting a horse-drawn cab, which was also damaged. The fireman was given a month's notice to leave the railway.

In 1962 I applied for a transfer to Reading diesel shed, but nothing came of it. However, I was able to visit Reading with another split vacuum pipe, and had to find my own way down to the shed. I walked out of the station, turned right and went down to where the cattle market was in Great Knollys Street, then down Hodsoll Lane under the bridge to the steam shed. I again reported to the Fitting Shop Foreman, left the pipe and had a look around the town. I went back 2 hours later, then caught the train back to Didcot. I got used to this, and would even leave the item there and ask them to send it on next morning on the 6.00am early train; a Fitter's mate would pick it up from the station parcels office and take it down to the shed.

There was always something to do at the shed. One job we had involved working under a 'Hall' Class tender, where the water scoop was bent. The fireman had been too late in

Young firemen at Didcot. The three standing in front of No 7032 *Denbigh Castle* of Old Oak Common shed (81A) are (left to right) E. Bradshaw, John Ball and L. Knapp. *Author*

getting the scoop up and it had caught a set of points, bending and buckling it. There was a set of water troughs at Goring, not far from Didcot, and another at Aldermaston; Goring troughs were 620 yards long, and the Aldermaston ones 510 yards.

This was where steam locomotives would pick up extra water for their tanks or tenders. The troughs were situated between the rails, bolted down to the sleepers. Sometimes rainwater would fill the troughs, or there was a pumping station near the line, which kept the water in the troughs at the correct level.

The fireman's job was to lower the scoop into the trough as the locomotive passed over it. Winding a handle on the tender lowered the scoop, and as the water was scooped up a mechanical float lever would rise sharply. If anyone was looking out of the carriage windows at the same time they would be soaked from the spray coming from under the tender through the wheels. The fireman would look for the end of the troughs ahead and should wind up the handle quickly, noting that the float was showing full. If the scoop was left down too long, look out! That is what had happened in this case

So, with the oxygen and acetylene and the biggest nozzle we had, we got the scoop red hot, then, while it was still connected, hammered the metal straight then set the measurement correct with the trough size. Three of us were involved, one with a hammer and sledge and bars holding the strain, I had the blow torch nozzle warming up, and Jimmy, swinging the 28lb sledge hammer, soon put the scoop back into shape. We then freed off the pins and the threaded screws by oiling, and made sure the scoop fitted up into its slot away from the points. Again we were all black and dirty, but we enjoyed it.

Another time I was put on the lathe to face off some piston cocks, but the lathe was huge – too big for the job. I had to learn, so I clamped the cocks in, set up so that turning was true, then, with the cutter face off, I cleaned them down. It kept me out of trouble and I was learning.

But some men were getting funny. I had a railway cap that I wore when I was under the motions to save my hair getting dirty. One day

I came into the locker room and someone had nailed it to the wooden seat. Nice… I knew who it was, so I found out where he was working and got a piece of metal, made it red hot, picked it up with clamps, peed on it, and put it in the pit. It stank for days. I never let on to anybody about what I had done, but I never had any more trouble again. I had my own back.

During May and June there was trouble at the hostel concerning all the railwaymen. British Rail and the National Union of Railwaymen were having a conflab over payments for hostel rooms. Some of the firemen were saying they couldn't afford to pay any more; the rooms were so small you couldn't swing a cat in them. However, a planned strike was postponed, although talks were still going on. Again, on 8 June there was more trouble about the increase in hostel rent. The young firemen were really complaining and arguing among themselves. The problem was that money was so short at the time.

As already mentioned, my brother Paul was a Fitter and Turner but only did fitting work in and around the shed, and also went out on breakdowns; Bengy worked with him regularly. I kept clear because I couldn't be with my brother – I had to watch my Ps and Qs with him! Paul and all the Fitters had their tool cupboards in the Lifting Shop along one side of the wall on the right-hand side as you walked in. Paul's mate was Bob, and he was a good laugh. Paul and his wife Joan lived up in Park Road, Didcot, above Mr Jenkins's paper shop, and Joan worked in the shop. Next door was Moxon's fish and chip shop. Well, Paul and Bob were having a bit of a problem with Dave and Jim. So one night Paul went to Moxon's and asked for a piece of cod, then went to work on nights. In the middle of the night, after the entire shed was quiet, they got to work. They lifted out Dave's tool locker – and those cupboards were heavy – nailed the fish to a baton on the wall, then lifted the cupboard back into place. They covered their tracks and sprinkled dust on the floor around the base.

After about a week or so flies started coming in and buzzing around, big bluebottles. Dave and Jim sprayed Jeyes fluid around the area; I did hear them say that something must have died. Then they asked Paul and Bob if they could smell anything. Bob was smoking at the time and just blew some smoke out and said, no, he couldn't smell anything. It got so bad that even Paul and Bob began to feel sick, so they pulled out the cupboard and there were flies and maggots everywhere. Dave and Jim went mad and so did Jimmy Tyler – what it had to do with him, I don't know. They sprayed Jeyes fluid everywhere and Paul just looked innocent, but after that he and Bob were left alone.

Dave always had time for the apprentices. He helped me several times to make things. I had a canoe at home, and to get it to the Thames at Wallingford, 7 miles from Didcot, Dave and I built a frame with a pair of pram wheels in the middle and an 'S' hook to connect it to the frame under the saddle of my bike. In those days there wasn't much traffic on the roads – you would be lucky to see six cars pass you. The frame was built from metal tubes, which we got from the carriage sidings where they broke up old horseboxes. Then I met with Bill, another Didcot boy, and he also brought a canoe, and we spent our time on the Thames, canoeing and swimming and drinking.

One Saturday night Mick and I went out 'on the razz' and ended up at the Chequers at Harwell, about 3½ miles from Didcot. As we walked into the pub, there over in the corner were the lads, Jimmy, Dave, Jim and Bob. Mick went to the bar, then up came Bob and bought a round of ale. We were invited over to their corner, so every time I got up to get a round of ale I was told to 'Sit down – you don't earn enough.' We then got into an argument and I was told to shut up. Around the pub everyone was buying tote tickets, and the prize was £15.00, so we said that if we won it we would have to sit there and drink the pot and share it. Guess what? I won the pot. Fifteen quid. I was handed a fiver to put in my pocket, and they let me buy the beer after that. What a good night we had! They caught a taxi home, and Mick and I walked home as happy

No 3440 *City of Truro* receives a polish outside Swindon Works. *Author*

as sandboys. The following Monday morning we all had a good laugh about it.

Meanwhile it was back to repairs and working on the locomotives, dirt and grime, and going over to the Parcels Depot to see Mick and Pete, and a chap named Brian.

We had 4-4-0 No 3440 *City of Truro* in on No 1 road at the end of the shed next to the Lifting Shop doors. It was going to work the Royal Train down the branch line from Cholsey to Wallingford. Young cleaners and firemen were put on it to clean it and make it spotless. First they cleaned off all the dirt with cotton waste and a steam hose, then there was a bucket of smelly soap to be washed all over the smokebox and boiler. This was then wiped down and left to dry. *City of Truro* was shining when she left the shed to pull the Royal Train. (This famous preserved locomotive achieved a claimed 102.3mph in 1904, then a world record speed.)

Mention of Royal Trains reminds me of a story about King George VI. Shortly after the end of the Second World War His Majesty was touring the West of England in a Great Western Railway train. Each evening the train would run onto a spare line at the local station and it was the Station Master's duty to look after the King and his party so that he would not come to any harm; he would use his platelayers to stand guard if there were not enough railway policemen available. As usual on such occasions the GWR issued printed instructions to all staff, carefully thought out to ensure that nothing could go wrong.

One night the Royal Coach was put on a spare line over which no trains were running during the weekend, and the Station Master took every possible care of the King. However, next morning things had *not* gone smoothly. Someone had overlooked the fact that the line was on an incline and the Royal Bathwater had not been able to fully run out through the plughole to empty the Royal Bath. The Great Western Railway had slipped up just once.

Thursday night came round again, and down to the Labour Club we went to pay our subs for the union. The yellow cards were handed in, then we had a couple of pints before going back upstairs to collect the cards

and see what was on. Jim Holmer, Dave and his mate Jim came in, so it was free beer again. They wouldn't let us pay because we didn't earn a lot.

On Friday morning, after a couple of hours of work, Bengy and I went off and got some carbide from the stores. We dropped it into some water in a bucket and left it in the corner of the room where the Boilermen had their lunch. They came out cursing us like hell and chased us out of their room. It stank to high heaven – rotten!

Occasionally on a Friday afternoon, when we had nothing to do, Jimmy and I would go out into the shed and wash the pits down, so that my Dad and Trevor May were able to get home early. It also helped to get the next set of locomotives in for Monday morning, still leaving No 1 road half open in case something had to go into the Lifting Shop; it was still only standbys ready to go off shed that occupied that road.

At night the shed was a different place. I always enjoyed coming in and out in the winter months – fireboxes, with their flashing flames brightening up the footplate, and the smell of oil, and hot steam blowing. I just stood and listened. Then I would suddenly jump as a safety valve lifted and blew the steam into the atmosphere from the boiler. In wet weather, the rain hit the boilers and steam rose from them. The Shed Foreman would be checking that the locomotives were coming in or going out on time. Bernard Barlow and Reg Warr, who were drivers, then Harry Buckle took tests to become Shed Foremen – you knew who they were, as they all wore bowler hats. Also they didn't stand any nonsense from Bengy and me, and many a time we had a talking-to.

●

There were breakdown boundaries around Didcot on the main line. Reading shed's area was up to Moreton Road Bridge, Swindon's was to Steventon Road Bridge, and Oxford shed's was up to Appleford Road Bridge. Didcot had more to look after than any of them, with the centre marshalling yard and the Ordnance Depot for the Army stores.

Thus the Swindon and Old Oak Common cranes regularly crossed the borders to help out, because Didcot never had the heavy equipment to lift items back onto the roads.

On Saturday 21 September another locomotive and a few wagons came off the road just inside the border at Steventon Bridge. The locomotive, 'Grange' Class 4-6-0 No 6800 *Arlington Grange*, had fallen over onto the railway bank and taken its goods wagons away with it. So Swindon and Old Oak Common were summoned out to help lift the locomotive and wagons back onto the line, as well as Didcot's breakdown van and men. If there was no cover, the shed runner was sent on his pushbike with a list of names and addresses.

Being September, I started going to night school again at St Birinus School, two nights a week. On Mondays and Wednesdays, 7.00pm-9.00pm, it was Engineering Drawing and Maths and Science. But I met this lovely girl and took her to the 'Coronet' cinema up The Broadway in Didcot. Her name was Carol, and when we came out after the film ended I walked her home. A fireman saw me and said, 'Hello, Pat,' and I never thought any more about it. I was at work a few days later and Brink was talking to me outside his office near No 1 road when Ted Ireson, the fireman, walked up to me and Brink and said, 'That was a nice-looking girl on your arm last Wednesday night, Pat.'

'Not me – I was at night school,' I said.

Then Ted said, 'It was a good film, wasn't it?'

I walked off, and Brink asked Ted some questions. Then I heard a shout: 'In my office, now!'

Brink told Sam, the office clerk, to get out, then he went mad. I was reported to Paddington and the top man came down to see me. I had to change. Dad also gave me a hell of a talking-to, partly with his belt – and Dad's belt hurt! I think my Dad got his grey hair from me.

After I had my talking-to from Brink, I think he saw that I was getting a bit bored, so I put in for a transfer to Reading diesel depot, but it all took time.

On Wednesday 3 October 1962 a strike was

called, and all railwaymen except apprentices came out. We therefore had to go through the picket line at the entrance to the station at Didcot. When I came down Station Road it was quiet – no traffic on the road, no one walking about. It was like a ghost town. There was also no traffic on the railway, no movement anywhere. I rode my pushbike into the station entrance where the taxi rank was. Men were standing in a line dressed in their 'civvies', and I saw a slight gap to ride through.

One of the men walked up to me, pulled me off my bike and asked me where I was going. One of the Fitter's mates from our shed, Jim, pulled the chap off me and said that I was an apprentice and he should leave me alone. There was one more from our shed, Bengy, to come through, and four or five more for Reading depot. The man said sorry to me.

That day we all had to be at Didcot shed, so we swept and cleaned out the workshop. We also cleaned the breakdown van and had our lunch in the van and read the MPII, 'God's handbook' for the railway maintenance inventories. We went home early in the afternoon.

In the next day's *Daily Sketch* it was reported that an apprentice from another depot thought he would be clever and take a 150-ton diesel engine home from his area where he was stationed. But because the whole of the network was on strike, even the signalmen, he didn't think about catch points being set and they found the diesel engine on its side near a signal box. The lad had gone and legged it; whether they found him, I don't know.

The Labour Club in Didcot was the branch headquarters for the union, and the railwaymen on strike got paid 10 shillings a day for one day only. Didcot was hit the hardest over the strike.

One Saturday night Mick and myself went down to the Railway Staff Club, where there was a wedding reception going on. We fell into step and made ourselves at home, gate-crashing the party. Helping ourselves to the food and beer, we were both asked by Tommy Edwards who we were. I said I was with the bride and Mick said he was with the groom. They looked a bit oddly at us, but we joined in

Mick and I have gate-crashed Min Phillips's wedding. In the background is young fireman Chris Galloway in his heyday! *Author*

with all the party and dancing and had a good night. It was the wedding of Min Phillips, a fireman, and Shirley Goodenough, whom I met again on 5 May 2001 at the Railway Staff Dinner and Dance – and she knew who I was! We all had a good laugh together.

At work I made my own tools. I made a soldering iron from a copper rivet from a firebox by getting it red-hot on the forge, beating it on the anvil, then tempering it slowly. Then I attached it to a lathe and drilled and tapped it out. I found a piece of rod from the carriage sidings, screw threaded, and fitted them together, then to finish off I fitted a file handle. I later lost it, but eventually found it in someone's tool cupboard (Dave and Jim). I still have it today in my toolbox. I also made pokers for the fires at home – I think the whole street had one. I know most of the drivers did. Blacksmithing was good, and I really enjoyed it.

Christmas came again, and it started to get cold like the previous year. I guessed we were in for more snow. But there was Bengy and me singing carols again for the shed, and again the door was opened up and all the shed men joined in. We wished everyone a merry Christmas and went home.

4
1963: READING DIESEL DEPOT

Snow fell over Berkshire on 1 January 1963, and again on the 3rd and the 5th – 15 inches on that Sunday. Blizzard conditions prevailed and all roads were cut off. There were long delays on the railways again. On 10 January we had more snow and plenty of it – 6-foot snow drifts all around. Temperatures dropped down below zero on 17 January and all roads were impassable by wheeled vehicles so people walked everywhere. Locomotives froze up 30 minutes after coming into the shed. Everyone was helping to defrost the engines; the ground was so cold that a drop of water froze straight away.

Locomotives were brought into the shed and the doors were closed – this was the first time I saw them closed. 'Fire devils' were alight in the shed as well as outside, but the shed stank with the fumes. Inside the Lifting Shop the forges was kept going day and night with all the doors closed and even rags pushed under the door cracks. We also put newspaper into cracks to keep warm.

Buckets of ash from the ash pans were left near engines to keep the Fitters' tools warm so when you picked up a spanner the skin didn't tear from your hands. On Thursday 24 January we had more snow and blizzards. The Army Ordnance Depot sent over 40 men from the 521 Company Troop to the marshalling yard to clear the snow from the tracks; they were from the Pioneer Corps. The River Thames froze and at Abingdon people walked across from one side to the other. William Press & Son, an Abingdon a

construction company, sent out bulldozers to clear roads.

There was a -25 degree air frost, the worst since 1940. Once again tipper trucks were being filled with the snow and tipped in the Thames to get rid of it. A train got stuck in a snowdrift at Churn Halt on the Didcot and Newbury line; the driver walked 2 miles to report his predicament. A diesel was sent out and it took more than 2½ hours to pull the train clear. The Newbury line was closed to passengers by this time. I remember that a locomotive got stuck in the cutting near Hagbourne Road at Didcot. On 31 January it started to thaw slightly and we all thought it was going, but no chance. More snow and frosts at night didn't help, and locomotives were still freezing up. 'Fire devils' stood at the water columns to stop the water for locomotive tenders from freezing. When steam was escaping against the snow everything looked dirty.

It was a cold year and the snow lasted until April, coming and going with frosts getting colder all the time – from -10 to -20 degrees – and the drivers and firemen were freezing in their cabs, huddling as close to the boiler as possible, but only the front of their legs gained any benefit from the firebox. Few locomotives had sheets between cab and tender – these were pieces of canvas from the cab roof held up with metal springs and wire. They dated from the First World War and used to be called 'Zeppelin sheets', as they were used to hide the glow from the fire,

A stranger in the shed at Didcot: 2-6-0 No 76081 was one of the new BR Standard locomotives, designed and introduced since nationalisation. Note the cover between the locomotive and the tender. *Author*

Didcot's locomotive allocation in February 1963

0-6-0	2-6-0	2-6-2T	2-8-0	4-6-0 'Hall'
2201	5380	6112	2836	4902 *Aldenham Hall*
2221	6309	6126	2842	4908 *Broome Hall*
	6350	6130	2852	4910 *Blaisdon Hall*
0-6-0PT	6363	6136	2893	4935 *Ketley Hall*
3751	7327	6139	2898	4950 *Patshull Hall*
3763	7340	6159	3819	4959 *Purley Hall*
4606			3820	5897 *Brocket Hall*
8720 (BP)			3840	6909 *Frewin Hall*
9791				6937 *Conyngham Hall*

4-6-0 'Modified Hall'
6969 *Wraybury Hall*
6983 *Otteringham Hall*
6996 *Blackwell Hall*

4-6-0 'Grange'
6824 *Ashley Grange*
6849 *Walton Grange*
6868 *Penrhos Grange*
6874 *Haughton Grange*

All were Swindon-built except that marked BP (Beyer Peacock Co Ltd)

which might be seen from the German airships.

The new BR Standard 9F 2-10-0s were built for cover; the cab roof went over the tender, and there were side doors on the tender, with a small hatch to get to the coal. However, in the summer they were sweatboxes. The ex-GWR 'Halls', 'Granges', 'Kings' and 'Castles' didn't have much cover, just these canvas sheets hooked up. But that would keep the heat in, and leaving the firebox half opened allowed heat into the cab.

On 7 February everything started to freeze up again and more roads were blocked by the cold weather. In Sinodun Road, where I lived, we had no water for more than a month, and the Water Board sent up a road tanker. It snowed again on 8 March – it was never-ending. One of our Fitters, Jack Dearlove, lived in Blewbury in Oxfordshire, and he rode his bike to work; on a couple of occasions he left his house at 3.00am to get to work for 7.30, walking all the way. Jack Junior was about 50 years old; he was a good Fitter and knew his stuff. I always liked working with him, and only once did I see him lose his temper. We had another Fitter who thought he knew it all, and Jack threw him out of the rest room nearly into the No 1 road pit, but all was settled after a few days. Jack Junior also did the inspection at the coal stage while Ted Powell and Frank Dowding were on nights. If anything had to be done, Jack didn't hesitate – Brink just had to ask and out Jack would go.

We also had Jack's Dad, who was 70 years old and a Boilersmith. Jack Senior would climb into a firebox, pull a little wooden box inside and a sack, together with his tools, and sit on the box hammering and chiselling the old copper studs and fitting new ones in their place. He would take off his shirt and sit there with a carbon lamp, smoking his little cut-off pipe. Fireboxes could be very warm if the locomotive fire had only recently been thrown out. One day I was passing his locomotive and heard a knocking, so I climbed up onto the footplate, stuck my head in the firebox and saw him. I climbed in backwards and we sat together talking; I asked and was shown the what and why of his work. It was fascinating to watch him. After a while I started to sweat and removed my overalls. The base of the firebox had gratings and bars, allowing ash to drop through onto the ash pan. Sometimes these bars got burned and melted, and they would then have to be chiselled out and replaced.

The snow was on its way out at last but it was still cold, and when I wasn't busy I would walk across the main lines to see my friend Mick Howard in the Parcels Depot near the Provender Stores. On one occasion, as I walked into the rest room I trod on something and my boot started to smell of burning rubber. Mick pushed me off whatever it was, and explained. He put an old penny on the belly stove to get red-hot, then slid it off onto a shovel and onto the concrete floor. He

Looking into the firebox: the projections on the front and side are the stays. The firebars at the base would often get full of clinker from the burning coal. *Author*

would then walk out onto the platform to load up the covered vans and wait to hear someone scream when he tried to pick up the penny! That would stop him, he said, leaving the chap with a penny mark on his fingertips.

The Parcels Depot had been built in 1864 as what was then called the Transfer Shed, only ten of which were ever built. The lines to the north were 'narrow' gauge (today's standard gauge of 4ft 8½in), which the Great Western often scathingly called the 'coal cart gauge', since the very first railways were built to carry coal traffic in horse-drawn wagons. The GWR lines to South Wales and the West were laid to Brunel's 'Broad Gauge' of 7ft 0¼in, so if you wanted to travel from Penzance to Crewe you had to change trains somewhere with all your luggage, which was a nuisance.

The Broad Gauge train came into one side of the platform, and the 'narrow' gauge train stood on the other side while all the transferring was done. The Didcot Transfer Shed still had part of the Victorian crane on the platform that was used to lift the heavier items from one train to the other. With the end of the Broad Gauge in May 1892 the shed was used as a goods shed, then became obsolete and was used to store road vehicles, then was used for a while as a Parcels Office. Eventually British Rail decided they wanted the land it was built on for use as a car park and were going to burn down the last remaining Transfer Shed. However, the Great Western Society quickly asked if they could have it and it was immediately dismantled and rebuilt in Didcot Railway Centre. The old woodwork is a fine example of Victorian craftsmanship.

On 17 February 1963 it was my 18th birthday and I became an adult with another pay rise of £1 per week, so I took Ted and Frank for a pint in The Dragon. This was the only time I was ever refused a drink – I was told I was too young. In all the years I had been going to the pub I had never before been asked my age until now. How quaint! I bought the beer and Frank gave me a piece of his Erinmore tobacco to chew, then we walked back to the shed.

●

Working at the front of the shed, where locomotives were ready to go off shed, was enjoyable; there were different jobs to do and we had to be quick to get the locomotives off shed or the Foreman would ask questions and get very annoyed. Many a time when we were working at the front a fireman would smash the glass tube that showed the boiler water level and steam would blow out onto the footplate. He would then have to shut down the valves above and below the gauge and fit a new glass from the stores, then reopen the valves to check the level of the boiler water. He would clear away the glass and that was that.

Bengy and I were now working apart. He was in the Lifting Shop with Jimmy – that was the idea, anyway! He was also often sent out to Reading and Oxford with broken pipes to be welded, allowing him to get to know his way around when the time came for him to go to his next shed. Meanwhile I had submitted another transfer letter for Reading diesel depot because steam was on the way out, and we seemed to be getting more and more diesels in the shed.

Brink came out of his office looking for Jim Holmer – it was his turn to be on the front of the shed with Matt and me. We had to get a spanner and go underneath and adjust the brakes on a 'Grange' Class 4-6-0. Matt and I went under the locomotive with the huge spanner, not like a modern one but three-quarters of an inch thick and 3 feet long for a 9-inch nut; we also had to hammer. Meanwhile Jim climbed up on the footplate to blow off the vacuum brake.

Matt and I did sweat. The water dripping from the locomotive might have kept us cool, but the ash pan was warm so we couldn't win. We adjusted the brakes and checked the brake blocks for free play. We also made a report to say that when the loco came back into the shed again new brake shoes would be needed, and what a pig of a job that was going to be!

Didcot only had four 'Granges' at this time, Nos 6849 *Walton Grange*, 6868 *Penrhos Grange*, 6874 *Haughton Grange*, and 6824 *Ashley Grange*; the last-named was at present away at Swindon Works. The brake shoes were not light, and it was a two-man job for

Two 'Halls' at the front of Didcot shed ready to leave. On No 1 road (left) is No 6933 *Birtles Hall,* and on No 2 road No 6922 *Burton Hall. Author*

one shoe. But that would be for another time.

Packing pistons on the 'Granges' was another part of our job, Jim on one side and me on the other, with Matt running around for stores. Another job was clearing the sand pipes of any wet sand (the sand was blown onto icy or greasy rails if the locomotive was slipping on an incline with a heavy train). Slipping wheels could cause them to move on their axles, occasioning a visit to Swindon Works and an entry against the driver on his record. We had to empty the sandboxes, free the pipes and fill the boxes with fresh dry sand from the sand furnace on No 1 road. The sand furnace took the moisture out of the sand, and was looked after by the shed's spare fireman, who also tended the stationary boiler. The sand had to be carried to the loco in a bucket with a spout (a bigger version of a watering can) and was extremely hot; it burned you badly if it fell on

your skin. We considered ourselves lucky that we had not been born 60 years earlier, when the sand boxes of the 'Kruger' Class locomotives were perched on top of the boiler and the sand had to be carried right up there. Those Fitters must have been tough.

While we were working around a locomotive doing any repairs, the driver would prepare it, topping up all the oil points with his long-spouted oil can, wiping away excess oil with his cotton waste and replacing the cork stopper. With his oil can in one hand and cotton waste in the other you can always recognise a driver in a picture.

The fireman was also busy. He had to swing the canvas bag over from the water column and fill up the tender or tank, and break the huge lumps of Welsh coal with his pickaxe and hammer larger lumps into smaller pieces to allow him to more easily shovel it into the firebox. Sometimes there would be 'briquettes' of processed coal, which were not so good and rolled around. He would damp down the coal with the prep-pipe, then clean down the footplate. He would also lift up the fallplate, which covered the gap between the tender and the locomotive, and wash any coal from underneath. He would be very careful to lift this plate at the end, as the trailing edge could be razor-sharp from rubbing on the tender for many months.

He would also clean the windows, fill the boiler from the tender, and watch the gauges to prevent the safety valves from lifting with a roar of steam. Then he would rake out the firebox, put the ashes to left and right and refill with fresh coal. The best coal was Welsh anthracite; Yorkshire coal burned quickly and the 'briquettes', shaped like eggs, would roll about. Other railways did not have the luxury of Welsh coal so their locomotives did not perform as well as GWR ones, which were better machines anyway!

On the evening of Thursday 21 March 1963 there was a derailment at Didcot station. Two parcels vans were to be attached to the rear of the 6.01pm Didcot to Swindon train, but when the vans were brought out of the sidings onto the main line they both derailed. The Swindon train therefore left without them, but it caused trouble on the main line as all trains were delayed by 25 minutes. The Didcot breakdown crew and van came out from the shed, put the vans back on the line and had cleared the site by 9.30pm.

The gradual run-down of steam, and the lines of locomotives waiting to go off to the scrapyards, made Didcot, and many other sheds on the Western Region, very sad places to be. One engine withdrawn in 1963 was 4-6-0 No 5025 *Chirk Castle*. From construction in 1934 to withdrawal she covered more than 1,401,530 miles, and now she was waiting to go off shed with sacking covering her chimney, so no birds or animals would make their home in the smokebox. Her boiler was empty of water, and her firebox cold. She was eventually hauled away with a few other locomotives all coupled together, destined for Barry scrapyard in South Wales. The locomotive that pulled the cavalcade would also be staying, and would not be coming back home.

Yet only three years earlier BR had built its last brand-new steam locomotive, the last of

No 5025 *Chirk Castle* at the rear of Didcot shed in 1963, destined for the scrapyard. *R. J. Russell*

the 2-10-0 9Fs, the most modern and largest of the Standard classes. No 92220 was the last built, and was named *Evening Star*. She was allocated to the Western Region. The most interesting point on these locomotives was the middle pair of driving wheels, which had no flanges so they were free to move over the rail. Like the 'Austerities', the clanking noise these locomotives made was lovely.

When you climbed onto the footplate they had wooden seats, some with leather cushions if you were lucky, and also back rests. The driver could sit forward with his hand holding the regulator and there was a good view through the side window along the boiler. He could also lean out of the window and look through a quarter-light glass window, which stopped flies and foreign bodies getting in his eyes. The firebox doors were slightly inclined backwards into the firebox with a shelf above them, on which could be put tools or a billycan to keep warm; it was also ideal for heating Cornish pasties when coming up from Cornwall!

The engine and tender all looked as one, as the cab roof went back over the tender, providing good cover for the driver and fireman in bad weather, but very hot in summer. The tender had a pair of iron doors to stop the coal coming forward. These locomotives were phased out in 1966, but in 1965/66 I saw *Evening Star* at Didcot shed, and what a lovely sight she was. I was as proud as could be. I drove her down to the turntable with the help of her driver, something else I will never forget.

The story of the locomotive's naming is interesting. A competition was held among all the Western Region staff to choose the best name for her in Swindon Works. Three people came up with the name *Evening Star*, which had been one of the sisters of *North Star* in Broad Gauge days, the GWR's first successful locomotives. Earlier ones had been much less successful as their boilers were too small, the fault of Brunel, who built them in July 1839. The cost of the original *Evening Star* was £2,475 plus £325 for the tender. She was withdrawn in July 1870 but continued to work until June 1871.

The second *Evening Star* was one of Churchward's four-cylinder 'Star' Class, built at Swindon in March 1907 at a cost of £3,180 plus £485 for the tender, which could hold 3,500 gallons of water. She was withdrawn in June 1933 and replaced by the new 'Castle' 4-6-0s to provide work for Swindon's skilled men during the Depression.

Often railway enthusiasts came trainspotting around Didcot shed, taking numbers of the locomotives along No 1 road after asking permission from the Shedmaster or Running Shed Foreman. I used to talk to them, then would return to the fitting shop, take out the box of metal stamps from the tool cupboard, find an old spanner or piece of rusty metal from the scrap bin and, with the stamp and a 2lb hammer, stamp 'GWR' on it. They thought this was gold!

Diesels were increasingly appearing on the main line. One day Bengy was sent to Swindon to order spares for jobs waiting to be done; he arranged for the spares to come in from Swindon next morning by train, and a Fitter's mate would pick them up and take them to the shed. About 9.30am the following morning Brink came out of his office and told Jim Tyler to get me and go up to the station as a passenger train was coming in from Bristol and the passengers were complaining that it was cold.

The train arrived behind a D8xx 'Warship' diesel-hydraulic, and we climbed aboard and tried to get the steam-heating boilers fired up. The spare driver said that we would both have to go with them to Paddington, so off we went for a day out in London. We couldn't get the boiler working at first, but near Twyford we got it fired up – the filters were blocked. We went into the rear cab and sat out the rest of the journey, but the noise in the engine room nearly blew your ears out. We left the engine at Paddington and Jim rang Brink from the Station Master's office.

'What are you doing in London?' asked Brink.

We explained that the train would not stop for us, but we had found a Didcot driver going home in a D7xxx 'Hymek' diesel-hydraulic. Once more we sat in the rear cab, still in our overalls. At some point we had to walk through into the front; this was good but again very noisy in the engine room.

In May 1963 I received my transfer from Didcot shed, my first move with more to come. I think Brink helped me because he knew I was getting bored, and I would now be out of his hair; perhaps he was finding me a bit of a handful. Anyway, Reading here I come.

Reading diesel depot accommodated diesel multiple units (DMUs), 'Warship' and D1000 'Western' Class locomotives, and 350hp shunters. My lifestyle changed: my clothes were cleaner, and Mum would not have do any washing of overalls for six months. The depot was also clean: the floors and walls were spotless. What a difference from Didcot! I worked with some good Fitters, as well as apprentices like Dennis, Jim Tyler's son. Mick Russell lived in the same road as me at Didcot, there was another little chap from Hendred, near Wantage, whose nickname was 'Noddy', and Mick Massey from Moreton near Wallingford. We had all gone to the same school, St Birinus, except for the chap from Hendred.

That month a memorial was dedicated to the 11 people who had lost their lives in the train crash at Milton, near Steventon, when 'Britannia' 'Pacific' No 70026 *Polar Star* came off the track in November 1955. The memorial was a set of iron gates at the entrance to All Saints Church burial ground at Didcot. Relatives and friends came from all over the country and thanked the Rev Eric Knell and the people of Didcot for their kindness and sympathy at that difficult time.

The locomotive had been working a Sunday excursion from South Wales. Whereas Great Western Railway drivers sat on the right-hand side of the cab, the driver of this BR loco sat on the left-hand side with his hand on the regulator looking out of the forward quarter-light window. He had not taken into account the notes he should have read regarding Sunday work being carried out on the track, involving the changing and building up of ballast under the track at Milton. He approached at 50mph, then heard his fireman shout out and saw the restriction signs showing a 10mph limit for the points over to the goods line. What else could they

Above 'Warship' Class No D802 *Formidable* at Reading Station in 1963. *Author*

Below 'Hymek' No D7071 at Didcot in 1965. *Author*

Memories of the Milton crash of 1955 involving 'Britannia' No 70026 *Polar Star*. *Author*

do but climb into the tender and hang on for dear life, which saved their lives. As the engine took the points at 50mph it turned over, taking with it a few carriages, and rolled down the embankment, killing 11 people and injuring 157.

My brother Richard and Jimmy Tyler with the rest of the Didcot breakdown crew were called out, as well as both cranes from Old Oak Common and Swindon. The cranes lifted the tender up the embankment and some of the least-damaged carriages, but the rest were like matchwood. The 'Britannia' lay embedded in the earth; men had to dig out around it, filling wheelbarrows and walking along scaffolding planks to dump the earth away from the scene. Removing all the broken parts from the locomotive allowed another lift at ground level, after chopping down trees and the permanent way gangs laying a new railway line from an existing line from one of the store sheds at Didcot Army Ordnance Depot to get as close as possible. The 'Britannia' was taken to Swindon Works, outside which it stood for several years.

Didcot shed gave me a free workman's pass for my journey back and forth, and on

occasions I used it for nights out at Reading. I was put with different Fitters every other week, to be put through the basic practice and procedures involved with services, which were Monthly, Quarterly, Half Yearly and Yearly. Mostly the work was on DMUs, removing the tappet covers from the engines and setting up the tappets with feeler gauges. They were AEC engines made at Southall, near London.

Checking tappets, belts, drives and gears, mostly on Yearly services, one gang worked

My workman's six-monthly pass to Reading, dated November 1963. The phone number was the direct line to the shed via the Paddington private exchange. *Author*

A single-car diesel unit at Abingdon station in the 1960s. The MG factory exported its cars worldwide from this small station. *Author*

nights at one end of the railcar and the second gang worked at the other end on day work. There were two AEC side-valve engines on each car, four engines on a three-car set. The DMU drove in above you, so working on them was easy; a three-car set occupied the full length of the new shed.

Steps were provided to get into the cab or railcar. I was put in the driver's seat in the cab, and was first of all shown the controls. The Fitter told me to move the gear handle till it clicked into drive, but I pushed the gear lever through all the gears in one straight move. The Fitters stopped the diesel engine and I was told to go underneath and climb up and over the torque converter to the gearbox, then remove all the nuts from the cover plate of the gearbox, which housed the driving sprockets, and inspect the inside with the Fitter. I was lucky that nothing was broken, or I would have been in trouble.

At break times we went into the locker room downstairs and washed our hands in the fountain and round washbasin in the middle of the floor. Then we went upstairs for our break, looking out over the marshalling yard and main line. I got friendly with a cleaner, we got talking and I remember he said that he was constipated, so I wrote out what he should take – Ex-lax chocolate – and how he should take it. I didn't see him for a week, then when he did come back to work he looked as though

he had lost some weight. He said he had eaten all the Ex-lax in one go. It certainly solved his problem! I couldn't stop laughing, and he joined in after a while.

At dinnertime I would hang around in the rest room playing cards or go to town with Dennis for an hour. We would walk into a store where a young girl was serving and make her blush and have a laugh.

One day we had a 'Warship' come in for some work; it was a job to sit on the driver's seat and look over the bonnet. Between the driver's and fireman's seats there was a small door into the nose of the cab. The engine room was behind the driver; a small door and walkway led into the engine compartment, which also contained the boiler for heating the stock when hauling a train. You could walk from one cab through the compartment into the other.

Myself and a few other apprentices were sitting in the cab having a laugh and reading the paper when a man came up the ladder. He shouted at us – really let rip! He was only the Chief Mechanical Engineer! He shouted at all of us, and we stood to attention. He never caught me doing that again.

All the lads from Didcot caught the 7.20am train and each day we sat together in the same compartment playing cards or talking. When we got into Reading station we went back to the end of the platform and walked across the lines to get to the far-side path. We then walked down past the West signal box and crossed the main line again to the steam shed. There were eight roads. We looked all ways, as this was the main line from Cornwall, many a time hearing a whistle blow. We were also careful not to step on any points in case they moved.

Once, as we all came off the train and went over to the path on the west side, one of the Didcot lads just turned round, walked back to the station, got onto the Didcot train and waved at us as the train went by.

One day, as I walked past Reading steam shed near the turntable, there was a 'Hall' Class locomotive waiting to be turned. I knew the Didcot driver, Harry Merrick, and his fireman, Roland James, and he asked me if I would like to balance the loco on the table. Of

Steam at Reading: No 7816 *Frilsham Manor* and (*below*) No 5904 *Kelham Hall* – note the daydreaming shunter sitting on the line! *Author*

course I jumped at the chance. I was with a few lads I knew and worked with in the depot. Well, I wound it into forward gear, opened the regulator slightly then shut it and applied the vacuum brake, but missed the balance. Winding it back into reverse gear, I let off the vacuum brake and missed the balance again. The sweat dropped off me. In the end I climbed off the locomotive and Harry laughed at me and blew the whistle. All my mates teased me and slapped me on the back. Later the locomotive came back down the road and Harry and Roland waved and laughed and blew the whistle again. I was laughed off the locomotive, and it has always stuck in my mind. I remember all the good times and grin when writing them down.

Many a time I had to go up to the station at Reading with a Fitter and fix windscreen wipers or crawl between the car sets and fix something or other. Another part of the apprentice's job in the depot was to mix the antifreeze fluid for the diesels. This was done in a side area in the depot allocated for the barrels of antifreeze/water mix. Also in the same area were crates of injectors for the diesel engines.

One Saturday night I went to Reading by a stopping train with a girlfriend. When we got to Tilehurst station someone pulled the communication cord; the vacuum brake came on, but then the train wouldn't move. The Station Master had to instruct the signalman to stop a main-line train to get the passengers to Reading. In the meantime I was asked to try to find the fault, but I couldn't, and a Fitter came out from the depot to fix the problem. I was told on Monday morning what the problem was, so if it happened again I would know what to do.

On Friday nights, on the way home from work, I would go down to Didcot shed and swap my dirty overalls for clean ones. On occasions, when the train came into Reading, Didcot men were driving the 'Hymek' that had come up from Paddington. The driver would shout from the window, 'Come up front and ride in the cab with me to Didcot.' To stand up front and watch the other trains coming at you on the up line was thrilling. As we came into Didcot station I was allowed to sound the horn, and there waiting for me was

Carol, an ex-girlfriend. As I went by I sounded the horn and everyone jumped out of their skins. It was very amusing for those watching.

While working at Reading depot I met some good apprentices. There was Dennis, of course, Mick Quartermaine, a Mechanical apprentice, and Dave Smith from Reading, an Electrical apprentice. Mick came from Tilehurst and at weekends he played double bass in a group around Reading. We would later meet up at Old Oak Common with another apprentice from Reading depot called Alan Brown who came from Newbury.

Mick Quartermaine was a skinny kid, not much fat on him, and he rode an old scooter, a German Zundapp Bella. He sold it to me and it lasted a few years before I scrapped it. We used to ride it from the depot down the side of the track, falling off a few times, across to Hodsoll Lane and out into Great Knollys Street and the corner shop from where we bought food, then rode back again. We were both idiots!

Once Dennis, Mick and I all went out up to Dave's house. We were a bit late coming back at lunchtime, so we parked Dave's van at Reading station and cut through the station. If anyone asked us why we were late, we would say that we had been working on a DMU at the station. On the way into the front of the station a little Navy Wren was lugging her kit bags up the stairs to No 1 platform.

As we ran by, I shouted, 'Carry your bags, lady?' and ran up the stairs.

She grabbed Mick and said, 'Here, then, carry these,' and Mick had the lot of them.

He called out, 'You said that, Pat! Come back here and give me a hand!'

So Dave, Dennis and I ran back down the stairs, taking a bag each from Mick. We ran back up the stairs and dropped them on the platform, then ran down the West signal box pathway to the depot. The Wren gave Mick some cigarettes, so he was happy.

As we all ran down past the signal box, a train came round the bend and we stood between two trains, frozen, till they went by, then legged it down to the depot, jumping over the points on the main line; these would move for the next train as the first one went past. We just made it into the depot back door and went under the DMU, making out we had been there all the time.

I was called into the office on Friday and was told that my six months were up. I was being transferred back the following Friday, and that would be my last day. So the following week we all had some good times together.

I recall that we met up with an apprentice who had just come back to his own depot from a transfer. He had a BSA 650cc Road Rocket motorbike and sidecar, so Dave, Mick, Dennis and I got on it with the owner and went up to Reading for a ride – Dave, Mick and Dennis were in the sidecar and I was on the bike. Five of us – it was all good fun!

That week I was asked to go down to Huntley & Palmer's biscuit factory where a D39xx 0-6-0 diesel shunter was having trouble with the vacuum brake. These were English Electric 350hp shunters – very powerful. Huntley & Palmer also had its own engine, a fireless steam loco, which was filled up with steam for its day's working, but if you drove it too far it used up its allocated steam and just stopped. Then it had to be pulled back into the factory to be filled up again. When I went down that day, it was standing across a set of points, dead as a doornail.

●

In November 1963 I went back to Didcot. Reading had been good, clean and tidy. We all said our goodbyes, then come Monday morning I was back. Bengy was still there, so we swapped stories and I said he would enjoy Reading when it was his time to go.

We were going out on more and more breakdowns together. I came into work one Thursday and was told to get oil, rags, tools and some sacks together as we were going out early on Friday morning on a shunter, an English Electric 350hp D39xx 0-6-0, to Moreton marshalling yard. A wagon with a 'hot box' had been brought in from a main-line train; the oil couldn't get to the metal bearing in the journal as the oil holes were blocked up, so it ran hot. The carriage and wagon breaker's yard was closing, so there was no one there to do this work, which is why the shed Fitters had been told to do it. We strapped and tied our jacks, bars, oil and tools onto the side of the shunter, then Jim Tyler, Bob Warrick and I climbed up into the cab with the driver and 'second man' (fireman) – there was not much room to move about! And we had not been given any footplate passes! Moreton was about 4 or 5 miles away towards Reading, near Cholsey station.

We were dropped near the wagon and took our tools to the job. I was sent up to the shunter's cabin to make the tea and we drank it on the job. We stripped out the bearings, fitted new ones, oiled up, dropped the jacks, cleaned all the tools and had an afternoon watching the shunters go up and down with

---

Didcot's locomotive allocation in November 1963

0-6-0	2-6-0	2-6-2T	2-8-0	4-6-0 'Hall'
2201	6309	6112	2893	4905 *Barton Hall*
2221	6350	6126	3819	4910 *Blaisdon Hall*
	6363	6130	3820	4959 *Purley Hall*
0-6-0PT	6367	6136	3840	6909 *Frewin Hall*
3751	6378	6139		6937 *Conyngham Hall*
8720 (BP)	6385	6145		
9791	7308	6159		**4-6-0 'Modified Hall'**
	7327			6969 *Wraysbury Hall*
	7340			6983 *Otteringham Hall*
				6996 *Blackwell Hall*

All were Swindon-built except that marked BP (Beyer Peacock Co Ltd)

their trains. We had to wait for a ride back to Didcot so we were told to get our tools and equipment into a guard's van that was going back with a train around the east loop to Oxford. The train stopped outside the shed and we dropped off our equipment and walked across the tracks – 5, 6, 7 and 8 – into the Lifting Shop, waving to the driver and thanking the guard. A guard's van was comfortable, with seats and a stove; it also had side windows to look out at an angle and its own balcony on which to stand.

For Bonfire Night 1963 I brought in some jumping jacks – huge they were. They cost about threepence each from Red Stores in The Broadway, Didcot. We had all heard about Bob Looms, who was a war hero and fighter pilot during the Second World War. Well, it was afternoon tea, and Bob was sitting against the sink with his strong, sweet tea, smoking his roll-ups – and they stank. I nudged Bengy to give me a light. Bob was half asleep, so Dave, Jim, Paul, Bob, Jim, Ted and Frank started to leave the cabin – quietly. I lit the jumping jack and chucked it onto the floor under Bob's feet. We held the door so that he couldn't get out – all we heard was screaming.

Jim Hale eventually opened up the door and I nudged Bengy inside first. Bob grabbed him and started to scream at him, then my brother Paul came in and said we were all to blame and told Bob to cool down. Bob was standing on the table jumping up and down. Consequently I had another talking-to from Brinkley, but I saw him grin. I never played up Bob again – I left him alone.

December was near and I said to Bengy, 'Let's go and have a drink in the Prince of Wales.' It was about 11.45am so off we went across the carriage sidings and down the tunnel under the station. As we were approaching the taxi rank by the island, we saw George East coming out of the Prince of Wales, so we ran, both ways, like two headless chickens running around. I hid behind a tree, Bengy behind a taxi. We saw George going down the tunnel, then went into the pub.

The barman said that we had only just missed George East, and we said, 'Oh, have we? If only you knew!' All hell would have been let loose if he had caught us; we would have been

marched in front of the British Rail management for drinking on the job. After Bob's incident with the fireworks and my jokes, and having been spoken to by Arthur Brinkley, my Foreman, I did quieten down a bit.

On 2 December Bengy was transferred to Reading for his six months' training. Meanwhile I had to work in the shed removing a steam loco superheater from the smokebox door end. Because the smokebox was full of soot and ash, Jim Holmer, Matt and I wrapped ourselves up with towels around our necks and heads, buttoned our overalls up to the neck and tied our sleeves and trouser legs with string to stop the soot getting into our clothes. We climbed into the front of the smokebox over the blast pipe (which blew the exhaust up the chimney) and put a socket spanner onto the studs. We then tried to undo the nuts, pulling down on a crowbar after soaking them with paraffin and oil mixed together, until they came undone, screaming against the threads.

Then we pulled out the superheater, which had split, and got a new one the same length – about 12-15 feet. Then we washed the studs again in a mixture of oil and paraffin, passed up the superheater between the three of us and slid it back into position, replaced the clamp, then put the nuts back onto the studs with the socket spanner and bar pulled down tight.

When we climbed out of the smokebox we were as black as the ace of spades with sweat and soot. We tried washing ourselves off in the Lifting Shop hand basin, and I got a bucket of boiling water from a locomotive and stripped down to my inner overall trousers, to get as clean as I could. Then we washed again with horsehair and carbolic soap, and rubbed engine gear oil into our hands and arms to soften up our skin.

On Christmas Eve Bengy was at Reading depot so there were no Christmas carols at Didcot this year. But we wished everyone a happy Christmas and I was let off early to pick up my beer at the Railway Staff Club for the family. Just before Christmas I had put in for a transfer to Old Oak Common, and Arthur Brinkley said, 'I will do what I can for you. Something might come up in 1964, who knows?' Merry Christmas, Arthur!

5
1964: OLD OAK COMMON AND DIDCOT: ANTICS AND ACCIDENTS

Once again snow fell on 16 January over Didcot and Berkshire, although the weather was not as bad as the previous two years. In the New Year, after the firework incident, I was moved into Arthur Brinkley's office. Sam was Brink's office clerk and I had to learn the weekly reports while an eye was kept on me. My job was to keep the records of locomotives and next day repairs, and to pull out the cards and check each record for each locomotive. I also had to go in and around the shed and coal stage looking for our own shed's locomotives, which could be recognised by the oval plate fixed to the smokebox door with the number 81E on it. All sheds had these identifying plates: for example, Old Oak Common was 81A, Slough was 81B, Southall 81C, Reading 81D and Oxford 81F. I also had to take messages and reports from other depots or send back reports. I would relay them to Arthur and wait for his opinion – and he would keep his eye on me. I enjoyed working in the office, because I kept clean, until I had to kneel down to take the measurements of the thickness of loco tyres. I kept my own records of these locomotives and the driving wheels and noted when piston and valve rings had to be changed. Brink was pleased, and I was learning; I kept his office and the records were up to date.

I went over to a carriage and wagon siding for some scrap metal to make tools. Dave taught me and we made some inside and outside callipers from some old plate, with plenty of filing as it took shape. I still have

them today in my toolbox. I also made a table lamp from copper tube and an old lampshade from a carriage, but that has long gone. All my tools I kept, and the memories from Dave, to pass them on to other apprentices.

●

I got my six-month transfer to Old Oak Common in late January. Bengy was still away in Reading and wasn't due home till June. I now had to get up at 5.00am every morning, Monday to Friday, and cycle down to the station to catch the early train, which was pulled by a 'Warship' Class diesel. The train had left Penzance the previous evening at 8.55pm and stopped at all stations, travelling via Bristol, to reach Didcot at 6.00am. After that it only stopped at Reading, then on to Paddington, arriving at 7.20am. I walked down to the Underground and caught the Bakerloo line to Willesden Junction, then walked the mile towards Old Oak Common, passing Walls's meat factory on the right-hand side. I went over the bridge to the railway works, passing Reg's café on the bridge, then down the slope near the great locomotive shed with its four turntables, each with eight roads.

On the first day I reported to Mr Diamond, Chief Mechanical Manager. On the way to his office, in the roundhouse I bumped into two mates with whom I had been stationed at Reading depot in 1963, Mick Quartermaine and Alan Brown. What a surprise we all had! Mick and I travelled back and forth but Alan stayed with a relative in Kilburn. Our work times were 8.00am-4.30pm for Mick and me, who were travelling, but for Alan it was 7.30am-4.00pm, because he lived nearer. Going home we had to rush back to Willesden Junction and Paddington to catch the 5.05pm Bristol train on Platform 1 to Reading, where Mick would get off, then Didcot. On several occasions I was asleep as the train left Didcot on the way home and I had to jump out of the moving train.

Consequently I went to Whitechapel in the East End and asked my aunt and uncle, Betty and Mick, if I could spend my nights there, giving them my lodging money. I would now just go home for the weekend on a Friday night, and be back for 8.00am on Monday, again catching the 6.00am from Didcot. Sometimes I left Didcot on Sunday night for London and headed for Whitechapel, then I was in London for the next day instead of travelling and rushing about.

Alan, Mick and I met up with some nice chaps. One was John Langstone and another Barry Hughes. They were from Acton; most of the apprentices were from Acton, White City or Harrow. 'Blondie' was another apprentice, but he was more like a professor, wearing his thick-rimmed glasses over his nose; he couldn't stop talking. At night we used to go out with them, or stay over at weekends and sleep on the floor, or go out all night drinking and to parties. I did invite them down to the country, but that's another story.

One night 'Blondie' took Mick home from work on the motorbike and the next thing we heard was that the two apprentices were in hospital with broken arms and legs. I didn't see much of Mick for a while after that.

When a train came into Paddington with a parcel for the Electrical Foreman or Mechanical Foreman, John and I would be told to go up to Paddington to collect the item. We would walk across the carriage sidings to find an empty stock train with a loco attached ready to travel down to Paddington, which was 3¼ miles away. We would collect the parcel then wait for the next passenger train due in from anywhere in the country. The train would stop at the buffers and the train engine would be uncoupled. Another

shunting loco would couple up at the other end of the empty carriages, bound for Old Oak carriage sidings, and we would ride back to the yard. The train locomotive would then go to Ranelagh Road to be turned on the turntable, overlooked by the backs of private houses. There the driver and fireman would check the locomotive over and top up the oil for the con-rods and the water in the tender. We never went to work up there. Alternatively, if it was an 81A locomotive it would go back to Old Oak for maintenance.

That was also how I got up to Paddington on a Friday evening. I would get on the carriages at Old Oak and ride the empty train to the station, then I was ready for my journey home.

I did notice that a lot of steam locomotives were going and more and more diesels were about, which was good. Ranelagh Road was turned into a refuelling depot.

I met a lot of apprentices – there must have been 12 or more at the depot, of all trades. On one occasion we all met in the amenity block to have our break with the other staff, drivers and firemen from all parts of the old GWR, Fitters and their mates, machinists, etc. All the apprentices sat together and a tune was being played on the radio: it was the Dave Clark Five with *Glad All Over*. We all erupted and started banging the tables and floor to the beat. All the other staff, having their break, went mad with the noise and the singing, and we got a telling-off and were told to be quiet. So we got up, walked out and cheered at the staff, calling them old women. They did bite!

In our lunchtime Barry, John and I went to Reg's café on the bridge. His mugs had a blue ring around them; I know because I still have one today in my house.

You could see all over London from Old Oak, which, with its carriage sidings, was a huge place, with railway lines everywhere, trains running over embankments and bridges, double-headers banking up gradients and main-line locomotive-hauled expresses on their way in and out of Paddington. It was a great place, and I learned a lot there. I worked with a Fitter on the first Sulzer diesel that came to that shed. It was on one of the side roads from a turntable in the shed, and the smell of a new diesel I will never forget.

Above A steam survivor at Old Oak Common in January 1964. '5700' 0-6-0PT No 9710 is one a small number of the class fitted with condensing apparatus for the use when working on the Underground. *Derek Everson*

Below Sister loco No 9706 stands inside the shed at Old Oak beside a 'Hymek' newcomer in January 1964. *Derek Everson*

Two views of No 4079 *Pendennis Castle* at Old Oak Common before backing down to Paddington to haul a high-speed Ian Allan Railtour to Plymouth on 9 May 1964. Unfortunately she was to fail at Westbury. *Derek Everson*

Old Oak Common shed had a machine shop and a blacksmiths shop. One chap, Fred Lazby, worked the lathe, and I remember that he had a picture above his machine of a woman and a load of birds flying around – but I won't go into the detail of the picture too much. He drove a three-wheeler Reliant and sometimes picked me up at Willesden station if he saw me walking into Old Oak past Walls's meat factory.

Also stationed at Old Oak was the 'Blue Pullman' diesel train, kept separate away from the Great Western shed in what was called the Pullman Shed. No British Railways employee was allowed near this train, as it had its own Fitters and people to work on it. These new trains came into service in 1960 and were built by Metro-Cammell with a diesel-electric power car at each end. There were eight carriages including the diesels, and only Old Oak housed them. Operated by the Pullman Company, they left Paddington for Bristol and came back the same day. They were spotless

The first Sulzer diesel I worked on was D1717, seen here having just arrived at Old Oak Common from Brush in 1964. *Derek Everson*

and I never heard of one breaking down. At Didcot station I once saw one go by, then, 5 minutes later, another passed, going down to Bristol.

Sometimes a Didcot crew came into Old Oak, and one Friday afternoon at nearly 3.00pm I was asked if and at what time I was going home. I said the 5.05pm out of Paddington, and I was in luck. I had a ride up to Paddington on a diesel, then the shunter at the station coupled us up to the carriages of the 5.05pm. I rode in the diesel all the way home, stopping only at Reading and Didcot. The driver and his mate swapped about at Didcot and I thanked them very much.

Some of the apprentices at Old Oak Common had only just finished serving their time, like Mike Woodhouse. He had a motorbike, an Ariel Leader, and one lunchtime he took me up Scrubs Lane to see someone, and showed me Wormwood Scrubs Prison. We never wore crash helmets in those days.

At the weekends, when I was home, Mick and I would go down to the White Hart and knock on the door at 10.30am for them to open up, then walk down to the football club in Station Road, play cards and have a few pints, then go home for tea. Then I would call on my girlfriend and we would be off to the pictures at the 'Coronet' in The Broadway. But I couldn't wait to go back to London on a Sunday night. Before catching the train back, I would go to Didcot shed and pick up my clean overalls, two pairs, one for the following week, and put my dirty ones back in for the wash. Also I wanted to see the locomotives and the new diesels coming out of the shed; a lot of the drivers were on training courses for the new diesels, as was also the case at Old Oak and Swindon.

In about April 1964 the last engine to leave the Ordnance Depot at Didcot was a diesel driven by Mr J. Mitchell; he also drove the train out, and then the gates closed.

Part of my job was working with a Fitter, servicing diesel locos – the D1000 'Westerns' and the new Sulzers built at Brush – working in the pit, draining out the dirty oil from the engines and refilling with clean oil; we had to

Above A 'Blue Pullman' train passes through Didcot station. *Author*

Above Five minutes later another set passes through. The Pullmans were built by Metro-Cammell with a diesel-electric power car at each end. *Author*

Right A 'Western' Class diesel-hydraulic at Didcot station in 1964. *Author*

check the levels in the gearboxes with a dipstick. We were also shown how to check the service sheets.

While having tea in the amenity block one day, a call went out that all crews required for the breakdown gang were to be on station as a locomotive had come off the road in the area. So all the men rushed out with their cups and food bags to climb aboard the breakdown van. It was stationed just outside the amenity block, overlooking the steam crane, which was being fired up to raise steam before reaching the accident.

My six months came and went quickly, and in June 1964 I would have to leave and report back to Didcot. But before that, one Thursday in May, John, Barry and I went up to Reg's Café for dinner. When we came out a Watney's Red Barrel lorry pulled into the layby at the Railway Staff Hostel. The van driver pulled out the sides and opened up the back, just like a mobile pub. As we walked by

we were asked if we would like a sample of the beer. There must be a god up there looking down on us, we thought. So we sat down on the wall and grass drinking beer, free beer, pints of free beer! All the passers-by were offered free beer as well. When our glasses were empty, the other two looked at me, and I went up and asked if there was any more. I was told, 'Help yourselves.' It was nice and sunny and we saw the afternoon shift come and go at 2.00pm. Then we made a move – well, the truck was empty, and we thanked the driver. Nobody missed us at the depot anyway, I hope.

The following week I left London and we all said our goodbyes.

●

Back at Didcot there were a few new faces and Fitters' mates, one of whom was a chap named Jock, a little chap, who always sat outside for

In 1964 steam was disappearing fast on the Western Region. This line of withdrawn locomotives at Old Oak Common awaiting the call to the scrapyard in February 1963 includes (left to right) Nos 6005, 8763, 8765, 8756 and 6020, the latter formerly *King Henry IV* but now minus nameplates and numberplates. *Derek Everson*

Top Also minus her numberplates and nameplates and ready for the breaker's torch is No 5065 *Newport Castle* at Old Oak Common in April 1963. *Derek Everson*

Middle Once a mighty 'King', No 6010 *King Charles I* is in store at Old Oak Common awaiting scrapping in May 1963. *Derek Everson*

Bottom These withdrawn locomotives used to take carriages to Paddington from the Carriage & Wagon Department at Old Oak Common. Seen on 10 December 1963, they are Nos 5570, 1506, 9704, 1507, 1503 and 1500. *Derek Everson*

Above and left In store at Old Oak Common on 10 December 1963 are two '47xx' 2-8-0s, Nos 4701 (*above*) and 4705. *Derek Everson*

Left The last 'Castle' to be built at Swindon Works was No 7037, appropriately named *Swindon*. Here it is in early 1964, withdrawn and waiting for the scrapyard at Old Oak Common. *Derek Everson*

Inside the great roundhouse leading from one of four turntables at Old Oak Common in December 1963 are No 6827 *Llanfrechfa Grange* and ex-LMS 8F 2-8-0 No 48474. *Derek Everson*

tea break in the afternoon. It was a sun trap sitting on that bench, and maybe five men would sit there with their backs to the engine shed wall. Bengy and I returned to Didcot at about the same time and joined them to swap stories, and have a laugh and a joke. Jock thought it funny to start messing Bengy and me about. So later, when no one was around, we went on No 4 road inside the shed, and opened a window after climbing up on one of the toolboxes. We then went outside and pulled the bench to below the window. We told a couple of Fitters to sit Jock in the middle of the bench when he went out for his afternoon tea. I had a condom and we filled it up with water and tied the end. I climbed up on the locker, Bengy handed it to me and climbed up beside me. Jock was supping his tea. When I let the condom go it hit his head full on, water and 'French letter' everywhere. He looked up and went mad, chasing us around the shed; we let him get close and when he thought he had us we ran away. He was soon out of puff, and afterwards we all had a good laugh.

I was put in with Jimmy in the Lifting Shop and Bengy was with my brother, Paul. We had some work to do, not much, mostly piston rings and valve rings. If the locomotive was booked out that afternoon we went like hell to get it out on time. We took off the ring of nuts around the cylinder cover and, with a crowbar jammed between the outer casing and the inner, pulled the cover away from the studs; it weighed about 2 cwt. At the other end we disconnected the crosshead, then pulled out the piston. Jimmy showed me how to take the measurement with an inside micrometer so we could find the right rings for the piston, which were hanging up inside the tool cupboard. I fitted the rings into the casing, marked the overlap – ⅜ inch – then cut off a piece. Sometimes it was so brittle that I would put the piston ring into the vice and clamp it shut on the mark, then, with a 2lb hammer, knock off the end then file and face off.

Jimmy and I cleaned out the carbon with a file, fitted with new rings, then refitted the piston by lifting it bodily between us and knocked out the gland packing. We reconnected the crosshead and fitted new packing. Then the outer casing was lifted back onto the studs with a smear of graphite paste placed around the piston cover. Jimmy could lift the cover back on by himself – he was as strong as an ox – then I helped by putting on the nuts and tightening them down. The same routine was followed on the other side, and the locomotive went out on time.

There was a nice cooking smell from the shed staff mess room as I walked past one day. I went in to have a nose, and there was a young chap in there cooking apples in their skins in a pan over the pot-belly stove. He said to help myself – there was plenty. I looked at him, a walking dustbin, dirty hands and face and he smelled high. I said, 'No thanks, I'm not hungry.'

His name was Roy and he had his own room in the hostel in Didcot, which was called the 'Polar Star'. One day a few firemen burst into his room and grabbed him, took him to the amenity block bathroom, where everybody bathed and only a curtain divided the baths, dropped him into a bath full of water and scrubbed him raw; his clothes were just ripped off him. He took the hint after that and kept himself clean.

We were also having trouble with another Fitter's mate, Jim Hale of all people – he was like Stan Laurel, the skinny half of Laurel and Hardy, in the way he walked and laughed. I got Bengy to help me pull about 25-30 feet of fire hose round the outside of the Lifting Shop. We connected it up to the water mains and filled the pipe so that the water just came out of the nozzle, then lay a brick under the nozzle at about a 45-degree angle, pointing up just outside the back of the Lifting Shop door. Then I jumped up and down on the half-filled hose. It worked well – just the right height – and Brink was on holiday.

We refilled the hose so it was dripping. Bengy was game and so was I. I told Bengy to jump on the pipe as I ran by and shouted 'now'. We were ready. I went into the Lifting Shop chewing a toffee. Jim asked for one so I gave him one and handed them around, to Tyler and Davis. By this time Jim's was stuck on his false teeth and I took the mickey out of him something rotten. He bit, and I ran out of the Lifting Shop through the small door and

The doors at the back end of the Lifting Shop: we set up the fire hose between the tin shed, where they kept the firebricks, and the broken windows. *Author*

he chased me. As I ran by I shouted, 'Now, Bengy!' and Jim got the full force of water on him. He was gob-smacked and was dripping wet from head to toe, right to the skin.

As I said, Brink was on leave, but Jimmy Tyler got hold of Bengy and me and marched us up to the Shedmaster's office for a major bollocking. There must have been another god watching over us – George East was also not at work. So Jimmy said, 'Do you want me to take it further or will you do as I say?'

We both said, 'Whatever you want, Jim', so he went outside and brought in two rusty metal bars and told us to file them flat and square, and we had to water-test them for leaks. We also had to file 'slippers', which were fitted underneath the front of the locomotive as part of the AWS equipment. After a few weeks – nearly six – we were both let off. Brink never knew, and aren't I glad? He would have hung me!

●

When I came out of my house in Sinodun Road on the morning of Friday 14 August 1964 I saw black smoke rising above the town. As I rode my bike to the station, a man got out of his car and asked me how he could get nearer to the scene; he said he had seen the glow from Reading that night, with orange and red flames in the black smoke, and had just followed it. I rode into the shed and parked my bike, then Bengy and I walked down the east loop line towards the Black bridge at Appleford and North Junction. There we saw fuel tanks turned on their sides and flames coming from them; the air smelled heavily of crude oil and fuel, and the tanks were exploding. The bridge over the line was only a footbridge, and was twisted like a piece of wire.

The fire brigade was putting foam over the burning tanks. We were both stopped and checked for studs in our boots and lighters or matches, and were told to stay away in case it caught fire again. Then we saw the Old Oak Common crane on standby on the other side at the Appleford end, and the Swindon crane this end on the loop line ready to go in to lift the tanks.

Apparently an ex-LMS 8F 2-8-0, No 48734, had been standing at the North Junction signal box and the signalman had leaned out of his window and told the driver to go ahead. The 8F had its front end out of the marshalling yard, but the train, which it had to be coupled up to, was in the marshalling yard. But instead of reversing, the driver put the engine into forward gear and drove out into the path of the 2.17am Esso petrol train from Fawley, Southampton, to Bromford Bridge in Birmingham, which was passing from the eastern loop line onto the main line. The driver of the petrol train was Stan Wheeler, the fireman Matt Fitzgerald and the guard Cecil Tolly.

The aftermath of the petrol train fire at Didcot North Junction on 14 August 1964. The photos show the scale of the accident. The railway lines buckled with the heat from the burning tankers, and the Swindon and Old Oak Common cranes had to remove the footbridge before all the tankers could be lifted. The whole area was covered in foam for fear of fire breaking out again. *Author's collection*

As the steam locomotive hit the tankers at least 12 turned over on their sides. A buffer from the engine entered a petrol tank and the oil ran like a stream under the ash pan, then caught fire. The driver and fireman of the petrol train ran back, uncoupled the rest of the train and got clear. Later, a 'tanky' drew the uncoupled tanks clear and they reached their destination. Being night-time, the shedmen went out on their pushbikes knocking at doors for emergency help all over Didcot, and detonators were laid on all lines to stop any trains passing the signals.

When the flames were put out, the 8F was pulled clear – it was totally fused together from the heat of the fire. After a few days it was dragged into the shed and pushed across the turntable to the buffers. Brass and copper were melted in lumps, the coal in the tender was burned, and the footplate was burned away – you could see under the locomotive onto the rails. The side plates above the cylinders were buckled and twisted – not a nice way for a locomotive to end its life.

Subsequently the 8F was dragged from the turntable into the Lifting Shop, its wheels screaming and con-rods sticking, making grinding noises all the time. The big double doors were then closed at both ends and we started work on her. Dave, Jim and I stripped the con-rods off both sides and with the small pulley crane lifted all the parts into the tender and roped them together. We then cleared out the oil holes on the axle boxes and filled them up with oil. We got some wooden planks, cut them to size with a wood saw and put the footplate back together. We drained the tender of water – or what little was left in it, for some had boiled away. We took off the metal cylinder covers on both sides and anything that was hanging off, such as broken pipes. Then we removed the valve guides so there wasn't any movement when the wheels went around. This all took weeks to do; the main tasks were to free off the wheels and axle boxes.

Eventually another locomotive was brought in on No 1 road and was coupled to the 8F. It pulled her out into the shed to see how freely she ran, with us oiling her as she went. I had to go to the oil stores and fill up all the oil

containers and get a load of cotton waste, then we lifted all the oil and waste into the tender, in case the locomotive should seize up again on its way to its home shed at Tyseley, Birmingham, for scrapping. There would be no more steam mixed with oil to produce that magical smell from this locomotive.

When the big day came I was asked to go with the other two, wearing plenty of warm clothes with food and a flask, to ride on the 8F as it went north to be scrapped, all three of us in the cab. The locomotive that pulled her was another Tyseley engine. It was an early start and a cold day. We went past Oxford and Banbury to Birmingham Snow Hill, then we dropped her at her shed and walked back to Snow Hill to catch a train back to Oxford, where we changed for Didcot and got in late. But what a different world it was out there – I only knew the old Great Western Railway.

About this time my two brothers, Paul and Dick, left the railway and moved on to William Press & Son in Abingdon. For myself, I sold my scooter for a BSA 250cc C5 motorbike, which I bought from Trevor Goodles in Lower Broadway, Didcot. I also now spent most of my spare time in the new 'Buccaneer' café, or, as we called it, the 'Buc', next to the Post Office. The 'Buc' pulled everybody in from the villages and towns; also the girls were a better choice. I was still with the same girl – sometimes.

Having closed to passengers in 1962, the Newbury line closed to all traffic in August 1964 with the help of Dr Beeching; his job was to shut branch lines that didn't pay their way, so down came the axe. The line had opened on 13 April 1882 and was important as a short cut to Newbury and on to Southampton Docks. When I was 10 years old and went to school at Greenmere, we had a school trip from Didcot to the docks. In 1953 troop trains from Didcot Ordnance Depot used the line to Southampton with equipment to be shipped out to Egypt.

From Didcot station the line ran past Jobs Dairy then at the back of Hagbourne Bridge and past Upton Station out into the country. When the time came to demolish the bridges, especially that at Hagbourne Road, the council had to call in the Army to blow it up

Above The Didcot to Newbury route had closed to passenger services on 10 September 1962, and this photograph of the line was taken in 1964, the year it closed completely. *Author*

Below This is Upton station, also in 1964. *Author*

Above The view of the Newbury line from Hagbourne Road in Didcot at the back of Sinodun Road where I lived in the 1960s. *Author*

Below '22xx' Class 0-6-0 No 2213, seen here at Taunton station, was typical of the engines that worked the Newbury line. *Author*

as it was built so well. Wallingford Rural District Council wanted Berkshire County Council to demolish the hump bridge, and when the motion to this effect was passed at the Rural Council's monthly Aldermen's meeting, Stephen Freeman said that the bridge was a notorious traffic hazard, not only for motorists but to pedestrians and people pushing bikes. It wasn't a straight bridge, but was skewed, and saw many a crash or bump involving lorries and buses.

Being a branch, only lightweight engines used the Newbury line, such as the '61xx' Class 2-6-2Ts, '32xx' and '22xx' 0-6-0s, '57xx' Class 0-6-0PTs and 'City' 4-4-0s of the GWR, and London & South Western locomotives like the 'T9' 'Greyhounds' and the Southern 'Q1' 0-6-0 'Austerities', also known as 'Dustbins'. The latter were built without any unnecessary fittings of any kind; the boiler was shaped like a tunnel, and looked like a dustbin. Working to and from Moreton marshalling yard near Didcot to Eastleigh and Banbury, they pulled huge and heavy freights. By 1962 a single-car diesel unit worked the line.

During October we worked on the safety valve of 'Hall' Class 4-6-0 No 4959 *Purley Hall* in the shed; built in September 1929, she was one of the older 'Halls'. After putting a 'Do Not Move' sign on the tender, we removed the safety valve cover and the ring of nuts holding down the safety valve with a snail spanner and a length of pipe, turning off each nut in turn. Standing on the side plate above the driving wheel, between us we lifted the safety valve up off the studs and walked backwards with it onto the cab roof.

Walking back along the boiler and sitting astride it with our legs hanging over the side – like sitting on the saddle of a horse – we scraped the face joint clean ready for a replacement joint, then did the same with the safety valve on the cab roof. This done, we walked back across the top of the boiler and lifted the valve back into position, replacing all the nuts as before and securing them. There was no 'health and safety' – it was 'hands-on' in those days!

Dave Davis was the only one who kept me in line. On Thursdays, with Dave, Jim and the paymaster, I would walk up to the cash train

(with its bullion armour box van) at the station with a briefcase attached by handcuffs to my wrist to pick up the weekly pay for all the men. There were always four of us. The pay clerk made up the money in the Shedmaster's office, then at 2.00pm the window hatch was opened to pay the men, who were lined up in a queue halfway down No 1 road one, holding their brass pay discs with their works numbers stamped on them. Mine was 388. When I reached the small window I handed over my disc to the paymaster and he checked that my name and number were the same. I then signed the book next to my name, and he handed over my wages and returned my brass disc.

In November there was another derailment at Didcot North Junction. D6349 was passing onto the east loop line for Reading when it came off the road; the cause was a brake fault on the engine, which caused it to stop very suddenly. A few freight wagons also came off, blocking the Oxford to Didcot line into the station. However, trains for Oxford were able to use the eastern relief line, passing the derailment and regaining the main line near Appleford Crossing.

Both cranes came out from Swindon and Old Oak Common to make the lift. The Didcot breakdown also attended and I was asked to go with the rest of the crew. However, all we could do was to help move blocks into position for the crane crew, then watch the lift. When it was completed and everything was back on the road, Brink ordered us all back into the breakdown van for the journey back to the shed.

It was a bad start to the day on Thursday 15 December. I went to work on my pushbike as usual, but when I got near to the Kynaston Road and Mereland Road junction – crash! – a work bus hit me head on. I went under the front wheel on the right-hand side, and my bike went under the left-hand front wheel. I was pushed along Kynaston Road on my back for 5-6 metres with the front wheel crushing my chest; to this day I still do not know how that front wheel never ran over me. My hands where free, and I was banging on the side of the coach shouting 'Stop!', which eventually it did. The coach driver went missing and

Cranes lift the derailed diesel back on to the line near Didcot Junction today.

A newspaper cutting showing the Swindon and Old Oak Common steam cranes lifting D6349 back onto to the track at Didcot North Junction. Dave Davis is in the left-hand corner, and in the centre is Jim Holmer, with his hands on the hips, Jim Hale and myself. *Author's collection*

another man got into the seat and reversed the coach off me.

My injuries were severe, but I was conscious all the time, and the ambulance men said that they didn't know how I had stayed alive. When I arrived at the Radcliffe Infirmary in Woodstock Road I was transferred from the ambulance to a recovery bed. This was the worst part that I can remember, when the hospital staff lifted me up and over onto the bed. I prayed that they wouldn't drop me – I felt like a bag of loose bones. My Mum and Dad came into the hospital and I heard the doctor say, 'Have you signed the paper?' My Dad replied, 'Yes.' I saw someone cut my right arm, although I never felt anything, then a

tube was fitted into the cut and I saw blood fill the tube.

I was given an injection, and was told to count to ten. I got to five. When I was being operated on in the theatre I 'died', but the staff resuscitated me, and when I came out of theatre I was taken into one of the side rooms in Cronshaw Ward. This was an enclosed area with glass surrounds, and again I 'died'. I left my body and saw a priest at my bedside. I saw the doctor and nurses trying to revive me, and I saw myself lying on the bed. I had two angels holding me up in the air; I felt the feathers and wing of one of the angels touching my shoulder. The room was light blue, and it was so peaceful and quiet.

Then with a jolt I came back into the living world. I was told of my injuries: one punctured lung, broken left pelvis, and all my ribs broken. I had carbon monoxide in my chest, together with internal injuries. A tube in my throat connected to the hospital's vacuum system was being used to remove the carbon monoxide from my chest.

I couldn't talk. When I woke up one morning and tried to say something no sound came out, so the nurse put her hand over my throat, then the sound came. I asked for some water. I couldn't understand what this thing was stuck in my windpipe and in my throat. The nurse made a plug from a rubber and put it into the hole in the middle of my trachea so I could talk. The nurses wanted to hear me say something, so they gathered around my bed, and when I finally said a few words they clapped and cheered. I had to have a lot of injections each day to keep me alive, and the doctors said that if I had smoked I would not have lived.

My Mum and Dad and family came to visit me regularly together with friends from the street. I also had several visits from Carol. Arthur Brinkley kept in touch with the hospital daily; he had to report to Paddington. I was in a bad way, but I came out into the ward from the annex on Christmas Eve, and stayed there till I was released. There were no Christmas carols in the shed that year.

6
1965: SWINDON WORKS

When the New Year dawned I was still in the Radcliffe Infirmary. My girlfriend Carol came to see me on several occasions. Then after three weeks I was released and my Mum and Dad came to pick me up and drive me home. I think I was lucky. I'd seen some bad amputated fingers, and broken bones. I got off quite well, I thought, at the time.

Dad had left the railway with Mum in 1964 and had moved to Morris Motors' Cowley Works at Oxford. Mum stayed at home, which she deserved, having brought up three boys. When I had my accident it nearly killed her, but if she had known what had happened over the last few years working on the railway with all the near misses I had, she would have really created!

I didn't go back to work till a week after my 20th birthday in February. Bengy was at Old Oak Common depot on a transfer and we would meet up later in the year when he returned. At Didcot the tide was turning, as more and more locomotives were leaving for Barry scrapyards and the shed was only for stationary locomotives, and the new diesels.

In the meantime, one of the nation's great men, Sir Winston Churchill, had died on 24 January. As I was on sick leave, I went with my camera to the east loop line to watch the funeral train go by hauled by 1945-built 'Battle of Britain' Class locomotive No 34051 *Sir Winston Churchill*. The driver was a Salisbury shed man, Mr A. Hurly, and the fireman, Mr J. Lester, came from the same shed. The train comprised five Pullman carriages and a bogie van, in which the coffin lay. It had travelled on the Southern Region from Waterloo via Clapham Junction and Richmond to Reading. There it crossed over onto the Western Region, passing Didcot on the east loop line and heading for the Oxford and Worcester line, then on to Long Hanborough, the closest station to Bladon, near Blenheim Palace, where Sir Winston was to be buried. All the stations were draped in purple cloth in respect for the great man and people stood in their gardens as the train went by.

One night Welsh Stan got drunk, as did many more men who liked living near the Railway Staff Club. There was a very wild white horse in the field nearby, and Stan went out and brought it into the hostel, walking it through the passage down to Trevor May's room. Stan knocked on his door and told him that he had a horse for him. Trevor, who was very tired, gave him a rude reply, so Stan opened the door and Trevor got a terrible fright when he saw the horse over his bed.

The Monday I returned to work from my sick leave in February I saw across the shed on No 5 road No 6937 *Conyngham Hall* with a line of benches alongside her from the cab to the steampipe. I was told that we were having a photo taken so that we could remember our mates in years to come, when Didcot R&M depot had closed. About noon, everyone was called out and I remember seeing men like Tony Neal, Ernie Paul, Tom Edwards and all the rest, who were on day work, smartly dressed. I stood in the middle on the back row

Sir Winston Churchill's funeral train passes on Didcot's east loop line heading for Long Hanborough station behind 'Battle of Britain' Class No 34051. *Author*

in front of the nameplate, with Tony Neal to the right of Cecil Dawson and me to the left. Two photos were taken because people were talking, and one of them appeared in *Rail News*, which came out monthly. Bengy missed it; he was still at Old Oak Common depot until 5 April.

I went back into the Lifting Shop with Jim Tyler. We had a very dirty job to do, which was to go under and in between a 'Hall' locomotive and its tender and remove the coupling bars, then remove the loco's driving wheels and send them to Swindon to be turned on the lathe. The wooden boards had to be lifted out of the footplate, then we went into the pit under the tender and locomotive to remove the steel wedges that held the pins in place. Jim Holmer knocked the pin up – he was as strong as an ox swinging the 28lb hammer against the crowbar, which I was holding. God help you if your fingers got in the way! Matt pushed the crowbar against a tender wheel, and Jimmy was pulling on the rope, which was attached to the eye of the

The newspaper article read: 'Like most railmen who have worked alongside each other through the years, some of the men at Didcot R and M depot decided they would like a final group picture to keep as a souvenir – something to remind them of those nostalgic days of steam.' I'm the tall chap in the centre of the nameplate on the back row. *Author's collection*

Those nostalgic days of steam

Here's the group the men of Didcot R and M depot were so keen to have taken.

DIDCOT R AND M CLOSING DOWN

DIDCOT R and M depot is closing down to steam and diesel maintenance, but will be retained as a signing on point for loco crews.

But the staff of 150 have been assured that no one will be dismissed as a result of these moves.

Shedmaster George East told Rail News: "The fitting staff are going to Reading R and M and the mechanical staff will be absorbed in the London division.

"One boilersmith may leave and take the redundancy settlement."

Like most railmen who have worked alongside each other through the years, some of the men at Didcot R and M depot decided they would like a final group picture to keep as a souvenir —something to remind them of those nostalgic days of steam.

So it was arranged, and Mr J. M. Loder, divisional movements manager, and Mr G. E. Hanks, acting divisional traction officer, joined the men in the group.

shackle pin. Once uncoupled, we pushed the tender away out into the shed and applied the hand brake. Jimmy and I then undid the nuts on the locomotive's spring hangers and on the axle boxes, then lifted the front end of the locomotive with the crane.

Looking up between an engine and tender, showing the three coupling bars joining them together. *Author*

I was called into Arthur Brinkley's office and told to go to Swindon next day to get parts for a job we would be doing. I was told that there was a train at 7.05am and I had to be on it with the appropriate paperwork and travel pass. Later, when we were having a cup of tea by the forge in the Lifting Shop, I heard a lot of a noise coming from outside – it sounded like diesels revving up. I went out, ran to the turntable and stood up on the sides looking across to the Provender Stores and saw the 'Blue Pullman' going around the loop towards Appleford at North Junction. What a lovely sight she was!

Next day I caught the 7.05am to Swindon, stopping at all stations. I walked down to the Works entrance and tunnel, showing my pass to allow me through the gate to get to the other side of the main lines, and hearing the trains going above me with a clatter – superb sounds! I had to report to the main office to get my paperwork sorted out for the stores. I was slightly shy having to walk into an office full of girls typing; when they looked up I went red in the face. I asked the only man there if he could help me, showing him the paperwork. This gave him a chance to get out into the factory and enter the Works. We walked to all the stores, collecting most of the parts for the job, which were placed into sacks and tied up. The larger items would go the next day on the 6.00am train, which stopped at all the main-line stations to Paddington; each station or shed had its own covered wagon or space inside a wagon, suitably labelled.

There was not a train home to Didcot for another hour, so I decided to catch the next train to Reading, putting my spares in the guard's van. I sat near the van in case the guard said something, but he didn't. We went past Didcot at speed, then a ticket inspector came through and I showed my pass. He told me I was on the wrong train. 'Am I?' I said, so he took my name and shed and pass number. He felt good about it, I was reported, but I didn't care – I was getting off at Reading anyway.

At Reading I took the spares over to the main-line No 1 platform and caught the Didcot train. As I got off, the Swindon 'stopper' came into Didcot – I had beaten it by 10 minutes. I never heard any more from the ticket inspector. What a shame.

I took the spares down to the shed on a sack truck and asked Brink if someone could pick the rest up in the morning at the station at 6.00am. Next day we got stuck into the work on the locomotive; it took us a week and she was ready for Monday.

At the end of February I was informed that I was going to Swindon Works in the main 'A' Shops from April until October. Meanwhile, Didcot's shed roof and smoke chutes were being refurbished. I became friends with a couple of the workmen, and was able to climb onto the roof and walk across, then onto the planks provided for safety reasons because the roof was of asbestos and was not too strong. I walked the whole length of the shed and looked towards the Provender Stores and Parcels Depot (the old Transfer Shed), then across the east loop line towards Appleford Road. The view was good. When I came down I was as black as the ace of spades from the years of soot and grime. More washing for Mum. That pleased her.

Next I went with Jack on inspections at the coal stage on a locomotive that had had its fire dropped, as Ted and Frank were on nights. I went under the locomotive in the pit looking for bits that were loose or had fallen off. Jack was in the cab checking gauges, the regulator gland and the gearing, and the linkage. We had to mark down what we found on rough paper, then in the cabin, where we had our

Above Railwaymen were issued with two free passes per month, signed by the Shedmaster or his deputy. Here are two from 1965 used for journeys to London. *Author's collection*

Below My Didcot–Swindon free workman's pass. *Author's collection*

meals, log the details onto the correct report sheets. When I was under the locomotive the main items were broken springs, and I also found a few brake blocks that were worn. They were very difficult to change, so I knew I was bound to have to help someone out to replace them in the shed later on.

The place seemed quiet without Bengy because there was no fooling about. We were beginning to grow up by now.

April came and it was time for me to go to Swindon. I missed Bengy, but I hoped we would see each other some time. I finished with Carol and was as free as a bird.

On my first Monday morning at Swindon I had to report to the Works Manager, having caught the first train out of Didcot, the 7.05am. Alighting at Swindon I walked out of the station and down to the Works, turning right to the main gate under the tunnel and again listening to the different sounds of the West of England main line above me – the milk trains, the clanking side rods of the 'Austerities', the 'Macaw' bogie bolsters, the first bogie, then silence, then the second bogie, and so on. Then I went up to the main office and the Maintenance Officer's office. I recall being frightened to death as I sat in front of him. I was told that there would be no going home at nights, and I was given a name and address where I could lodge. His office was as cold as the North Pole.

I didn't know Swindon well. I walked into Faringdon Road but went the wrong way. I felt I was wasting my time, so I turned around and walked back into the town, past the museum. I found a row of Victorian cottages made of Cotswold stone. In its early days Swindon Works needed more and more experienced workmen who could not be recruited from the Wiltshire farmyards. Some came from the north and some from Wales, but the Great Western Railway had no accommodation to offer them; it had no money with which to build cottages, or even a refreshment room for the new station.

Then a London builder called Rigby, who had done some work at Swindon, offered to build 300 cottages free of charge if the GWR would also allow him to build the refreshment rooms at his own expense and operate them himself, keeping the profits. All he asked of the GWR was that all passenger trains must stop for 10 minutes to allow the passengers time to buy food and drink, and that no other refreshments were to be sold on any other station on the line.

The Directors were delighted and agreed to the terms. Rigby soon sold his rights to another firm for a very handsome profit, and that firm did the same, and so on. The soup served was so hot that the passengers had to abandon the rest of their meals, so Rigby did very well indeed, as the meals had already been paid for. Also, the quality of the food was very poor; indeed, Brunel himself declined to eat there. Many passengers began to refer to Swindon as 'Swindledon'.

The Great Western Railway began running mail trains through the night for the Post Office, which owned the GPO vehicles in the train. One passenger coach was included for ordinary passengers. The refreshment room owners took the GWR to court for breach of the agreement, as it did not stop these trains for the stipulated 10 minutes. The court decided in favour of the railway company, saying that this was a mail train under the control of the Post Office; it was not a passenger train.

Eventually, in 1895 the GWR bought back the refreshment rooms for a very large sum of money, as it was in competition with the LSWR for trains between Plymouth and London and could no longer bear to have to stop for the 10 minutes.

One of Rigby's cottages, the fourth from the museum on the corner of Faringdon Road, was the one I was looking for; it had a short garden at the front like all the others. (Most of these cottages still stand, as they were well built.) They had no bathrooms – those came later. Mine had an outside loo but no back garden, only a coal shed. I walked up to the door and knocked. Mrs Curtis answered and showed me where I was to sleep, in a room with four beds. Four different apprentices, all from different sheds and stations.

I recall that one of the apprentices came from the Rhondda in Wales. He said he would go back to the Rhondda; he would leave after his time and go back to become a dentist. He used to do all his own dentistry by looking in a mirror. I felt sick watching him. We all had our own keys to get in, and although there were four of us living in the same room, only two were there at a time as we alternated on nights and days. At meal times we had tinned luncheon meat fried or battered every night. I suddenly went off luncheon meat, but Mrs Curtis was a good sort.

You knew what time you had to get up in the morning, and if you heard the second hooter you were late. That was 7.30am. I had an alarm clock that I set for 6.30am. I had breakfast, picked up my sandwiches – Mrs Curtis made them, cheese or cheese and luncheon meat – then walked in through the tunnel with all of Swindon, up the other side, turned left and into the main 'A' Shop. Luckily I walked up with Taffy on that first day and he put me right.

I was taken up the metal grating stairs into the Workshop Supervisor's office, given my new wage and tag number – AE 0332 – and introduced to the Chargehand. I was then given a locker, pulled on my overalls and was taken around the plant. I was shown where I had to clock in and out, and was asked if I would work nights. I said I would. Then I was taken to a man who had just completed his apprenticeship. I forget his name.

'A' Shop was huge. It had a two traversers, which moved diesel engines and parts from bay to bay. There were no steam engines in 'A' Shop, only diesels – 'Warships', 'Westerns', 'Hymeks' and 350hp 0-6-0 shunters. Some with no bogies stood on metal blocks; some had all the covers removed and cabs missing. When a diesel was finished the painters took it away to be resprayed and transfers applied to finish the job, after which it would be taken outside on the traverse to be checked over for any tiny faults.

Besides the traversers there were overhead cranes running up and down, carrying diesels complete to their bays. The work was good and it was clear how important it was. The hooter always sounded to indicate tea breaks, when the canteen staff brought the food trolleys round, dinnertime, and when we had to start work again. Finishing time was 4.30pm, so it was back to the lodgings for tea.

Right Swindon's 'A' Shop in later years. Shunters are being stripped out and rebuilt. *Derek Everson*

Right The 1935 reproduction of the Broad Gauge loco *North Star* that stood in Swindon Works near my locker. It is now in Swindon's STEAM Museum. *Author*

Then bath night came. I went across the road to the swimming pool where there were baths partitioned off from one another, and waited with other men for a bath to become free. Someone would go in and clean the bath before it was used, and we had to hire a clean towel, which, with the bath, cost about a shilling. The enamel baths were all in a row and the water was very hot, so I had a good soak.

Thursday was payday. The cash and the pay table were brought out into the middle of the lower workshop where we clocked in and out. The table was wooden with four legs, and at the base of each leg was another piece of wood to raise it up. I will always remember that table – I expect all the men who worked at Swindon will remember it! About 200 men make a lot of noise, so you had to listen for your number to be shouted. Then you walked up, showed your disc to match your number in the pay book, signed your signature against your name, and were given your pay packet for the week. Every Thursday was the same – it was a good job I wasn't deaf, or I would never have been paid. If you missed your number you had to wait until last – they wouldn't wait for you. When we worked nights, the supervisor kept our pay for when we came in to work on the Thursday night shift.

Above where we sat to have our breaks, on both day and night shifts, there was an old

'Broad Gauge' locomotive on a stand, the *North Star*. On the other side, the turners were operating lathes, turning driving wheels and their journals with great precision. There was a crazy electrician there – somehow I always seemed to get involved with them, I don't know why. This 'sparky' had been demobbed from the RAF. One day I was in the nose of a 'Warship' Class diesel pulling some pipes or wires out of the way. It went quiet and no one was about, then I felt my bum go cold with a big rush and noise from the CO_2 injector fire canister. I was covered in ice and frost. My turn to get my own back would come – like an elephant, I never forgot. Everyone on the job roared with laughter while I crawled out brushing off the frost, shaking my head at this 'sparky' and calling him a prat.

Another job was removing the water feed pipes from the radiator of a 'Hymek' diesel. As I pulled out each pipe I labelled the end so it could be correctly located when the time came to refit them. That took a day and a half. Then I went with another Fitter to a 350hp diesel shunter to help him put the drive belts on to operate the generator. Then I was recalled back to my original job with my own Fitter.

On Friday nights I would run to the station via the Works path. The 5.00pm Didcot train left from the same side, and if I missed it the next was at 7.00pm. I would tell Mrs Curtis that I would not be back until Monday evening, and gave her my £4 10s 0d lodging money on the Thursday evening.

On Saturday 8 May 1965 I got up early and went down on my pushbike to the 'Buccaneer' café for a coffee and to see who was about. I met Jennifer, a nice-looking girl from Blewbury near Didcot, and we are still together today.

When I returned to Swindon for work on Monday morning, I rode my 250cc BSA motorbike. I now started my training, which lasted for a month, and was ordered to report to the supervisor's office up the iron grating stairs overlooking 'A' Shop. The following Monday I reported to the welding school by the time clock. This was new and it was good to learn something different. The crew of six included a couple of apprentices plus a carriage and wagon welder taking his tests; he was from the Carriage Department at Old Oak Common. Four of us were aged about 20; one was the 'teacher's pet' and motorbike mad, but didn't have a bike – he only read about them.

Back at my digs I had a heart-to-heart talk with my landlady, and told her I needed to go home on some Thursday evenings, so she gave me back some lodging money, which was very nice of her. After being paid on Thursday afternoon, I would run down to the station past the carriage works and just catch the 5.00pm for Didcot, when I wasn't on my bike. When I got home I would go and see Jen at home for a few hours, then go back to Swindon next morning on my bike.

Then, what a surprise, on 24 May Bengy came to Swindon and for six months stayed with me at the same house. He was in 'A' Shop too and in the same work area, but we seemed to miss each other as we worked different shifts. I was learning about welding in the welding bay with all the leathers on for protection, welding two plates together then putting them under a press protected by a guard, and pumping down onto the plates so they broke in half. This was to see how the weld and the welding rod had performed in the correct position, and to see that there was no flaw in the weld.

Every Friday 'teacher's pet' kept running to the instructor about the five men left in the training room. We got fed up with this. One day the tutor went for his lunch and the 'pet' went out, but he left his motorbike magazine in his welding bay. When he came back, he couldn't find it to read. I told him it was among the metal plates on his bench, but he still couldn't find it. 'No,' I said, 'in between the metal plates,' which were built like a pyramid. He took the pyramid to the press and had a hell of a job to split the weld, but he got there. I'd welded it quite well, I thought! When he finally opened up the metal plates there were only ashes. Of course, when being welded it had caught fire. 'Ashes to ashes'. He was choked, but he never went to creep any more after that. He also asked who had done it, and we all said, 'Us.'

I left the welding school having passed my course and went back to work on the diesel engines. We were working on a 'Warship', the one I had been on before going into the welding school, and the same 'sparky' had his head down a hole pulling some wires through to the engine. Well, I couldn't resist it. I stuck a CO_2 injector fire canister up his trousers and pulled the trigger. He kicked up and reported me, so I was taken into the office. We were both told off, but him more so because he was older, and was always fooling about.

One Thursday afternoon, payday, I heard two or three older men talking about someone who had pinched some bronze ingots, and they went over to the man who had done it and told him to stop stealing, and to go in and say he wouldn't do it again. He just shrugged his shoulders. As we were being paid, this man went up for his wages and two railway policemen came out of an office and took him away. Everyone looked on in amazement – we were gob-smacked and very quiet!

The wages for apprentices were good, as we got a percentage of the Fitter's piecework rate, so I was rolling in money, plus shift allowance. I did miss it when the time came to go back to my own shed. On one occasion when I went back to Didcot, and it was partly closed down and all the locomotives were leaving to go to Barry scrapyard, I saw No 92220 *Evening Star* all painted up in Great Western colours standing over on No 4 road inside the shed.

●

Working in 'A' Shop is was easy to imagine it in the days of steam, with railwaymen working day and night manufacturing and assembling parts with bolts, nuts and rivets, with the air guns banging away noisily on the assembly road. In 1939 a new locomotive is beginning to come alive, with a feeling in the metal that this engine will travel far and wide. The boiler is formed in another area, and the boilermen rivet every part together, then slide the tubes into place through the smokebox door and over the blastpipe, with the boiler inspector crawling into the new firebox to check that everything is correct.

Meanwhile the machinists are turning the loco's wheels on the great lathes, cutting each with great precision to the nearest thou, according to the plans. Heavy parts are being lifted and moved from all over the Works, the overhead cranes, in constant use, lowering their loads into the assembly area, with internal transport bringing in more items. Side rods and connecting rods for both sides lie on small blocks of wood so that they can be lifted up easily without catching someone's fingers. The edges have been taken off by a file, then oiled to stop them rusting.

The main frame now stands on the road on its axles with men crawling under and over, tightening down the springs and getting everything ready to lift the boiler into position and secure it with the big heavy air guns and hammers. Once complete, the traversing trolleys ride up the middle of the factory to the bay where the newly formed locomotive is standing. Locked into position, the men on the traversing trolley go about their work to winch the engine onto it. The trolley moves out into the open air so the tender can be connected to the new locomotive.

The men stand back, pleased at what they have achieved. With pride they shake hands, grins on their faces and pleased with the work they have carried out. A name is chosen from a book of 'Manors', and a number allocated. *Frilsham Manor*. No 7816.

With water and coal in the tender, the shed driver and fireman are on station and the engine is fired up. The warmth in the metal is bursting to bring the locomotive alive before being put through her tests out on the road. After the local tests in the yard, the driver and fireman and testers climb upon the footplate, get the all clear from the signal box and proceed onto the main line towards Chippenham for speed trails. Reading gauges and taking notes, they then return to the Works to complete the logbook.

The papers signed, *Frilsham Manor* goes out onto the Great Western Railway.

As the years pass, No 7816 lives through the Second World War, dodging bombs and bullets pulling coaches over thousands of miles. Eventually it is reduced to humbler freight duties. In the mid-1960s it finds itself transferred to Didcot shed, its green livery discoloured and blackened with grease and oil. At Didcot the metal starts to die and go cold.

And so, on 14 June 1965, a quarter of a century after emerging from Swindon Works, *Frilsham Manor* became the last engine to leave Didcot shed, pulling two other cold engines on the final journey to Barry scrapyard in South Wales. And, with great sorrow, Didcot shed is closed.

●

The newspaper report of the last steam locomotive leaving Didcot shed. No 7816 is on No 3 road on a Sunday morning with the last remaining staff. The Acting Shedmaster and Running Foreman was Arthur Leaworthy. *Author's collection*

The Steam Age ends at Didcot

A locomotive pulls out of Didcot shed: a familiar sight for more than 21 years, but one which will never be seen again. For this 78 class engine was one of the last three steam locomotives at the shed, and all three departed for the last time on Sunday.

Didcot locomotive shed was closed to steam engines on Sunday when its last three engines left for Oxford just before mid-day.

Built in 1934, the shed was used as a running and maintenance shed. And in its most active days between 300 and 350 men worked there.

Although the shed is now closed to steam engines, about 100 footplate men and 12 others will keep it open as a relieving point for diesel engines, and it will be manned 24 hours a day.

"There is no redundancy at all, said Mr. Arthur Leaworthy, of 128 Oxford Crescent, Didcot, the running foreman and acting shedmaster.

"Many of the younger men have left for other jobs and some of the older men have retired."

The closing down of the shed began about 18 months ago and up to last week there were 18 steam engines there.

"At one time we had over 65 here," said Mr. Leaworthy.

Mr. Arthur Leaworthy, acting shedmaster at Didcot.

Like the 'Manors' 20 years earlier, the D800 'Warship' Class diesels was built and designed at Swindon in 1958, and I was pleased that one of them, D827, was named *Kelly*! Eventually the 'Warship' I had been working on was traversed out onto the capstan and pulled outside to be towed down and fuelled up, painted and the transfers fitted. Once

outside with a driver in the seat, I was privileged to be asked to go out on trials on the main line with the inspector and fitters. We had to take the readings in the engine room of the revs from the engines on the run down towards Bristol. We swapped on the way back and took the readings in the cab. We were clocking 120mph on the straight to test the 'dead man's handle' and see if it would slow the engine down on overspeed, which it did. Then it was back into 'A' Shop for a check-over and to make out the report sheets.

Bengy and I met outside the workshops and took some photos of each other. I enjoyed Swindon and felt it was a pity to go home in October. I was sent a transfer memo dated 15 September, but because Didcot was closing I asked if I could go back to Old Oak Common, my second favourite shed. A further memo dated 5 October confirmed this, starting on the following Monday, 11 October 1965. Didcot was finished and it was a great shame.

Didcot's locomotive allocation in May 1965

2-6-2T	4-6-0 'Hall'	4-6-0 'Modified Hall'
6136	4962 *Ragley Hall*	6961 *Stedham Hall*
6145	6910 *Gossington Hall*	6963 *Throwley Hall*
6159	6921 *Borwick Hall*	6983 *Otteringham Hall*
	6928 *Underley Hall*	6991 *Acton Burnell Hall*
	6937 *Conyngham Hall*	7917 *North Aston Hall*
	6953 *Leighton Hall*	

4-6-0 'Manor'
7814 *Fringford Manor*
7816 *Frilsham Manor*
7829 *Ramsbury Manor*

Swansong of the 'Halls': No 6999 *Capel Dewi Hall*, built in February 1949, is on the early morning 5.45am parcel train from Paddington near Uffington on 17 June 1965. An ex-fireman gave me this picture. *Author's collection*

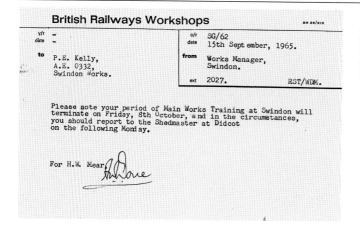

The end of my time at Swindon. Because Didcot was closing down I asked to be transferred to Old Oak Common. Happily, this was agreed, and I was to return there on 11 October 1965. *Author's collection*

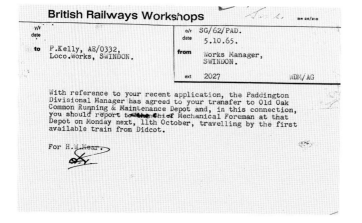

All the Fitters and their mates were transferred to Reading to work.

On that Monday morning I again caught the 6.05am train to Paddington, then took the Underground to Willesden Junction, walked past Walls's meat factory, over the bridge past Reg's Café, and down to the shed. What a sight! The main shed was being knocked down.

I had to report to Mr Diamond ('Legs'), the Chief Mechanical Engineer. The apprentices had nicknamed him 'Legs' after the American gangster, but you never said it to his face. 'Legs' asked me if I would work nights, but I declined with thanks. When I came out of my time there would be plenty of shift work to do.

That day I bumped into Barry Hughes and John Langstone again. They did not know I was being stationed at the shed so it was a surprise to them. I also met two lads from Glasgow, who were both on shift work and both stayed at the hostel at the top of the hill.

Steam locomotives were now being phased out at Old Oak; there wasn't much about, only diesels of all sorts. The machine shop was gone, and the blacksmith's shop. I missed Fred's picture of his dicky birds. All the eight main roads ran into the factory about where Fred Lazby's lathe had originally stood; there was a lifting bay to remove the bogies from locomotives. There were big changes at the shed, and they were for the better.

I went over to Whitechapel to see if I could stay with my aunt and uncle again during the week, going home at weekends, or so I thought. In fact, I never went home at all – I was in London and enjoying myself too much.

Bengy and I didn't meet again after Swindon. I found out that he had been transferred to Didcot on 24 October, then to

Oxford National Carriers Ltd on 8 November for six months. I didn't see him again till 1968, and then not till August 2002, when I drove to Cornwall and we met up!

Next morning I reported for work and had to climb into a D63xx Class diesel-hydraulic locomotive where a gang was taking out an engine, as a piston had blown through the side of the casing. The engine was hooked up ready to be lifted by the overhead crane, built by Vaughan & Sons of Manchester with a 30-ton lifting capacity. A Fitter and myself were up to our arms in dirt and grime, removing all the parts from the main frame. Another gang was doing the same on the other side. There were two diesel engines in each loco, and they must have weighed about 25-30 tons each.

The driver of the crane started the lift, but then we stopped him as we saw something still hooked up. This we removed, then gave the signal to lift again. Up went the diesel engine into the air, slowly. Then about 10 feet up we saw the chains slip – I was pushed to the floor and the other fitter jumped as well. The engine missed us, thank God; it slipped off its chains and crashed back into the belly of the loco. The chains were replaced correctly and the engine was eventually lifted out onto the floor. The filter casings were broken from the fall, but who cared – no one had been hurt.

After work we had a shower in the changing rooms, and that evening we went out with the Scottish lads. I always remember going into a pub and asking for three pints of beer and three whiskies. Then a bottle came out of one of the Scottish lads' pockets and refilled the glasses! The barman sorted us out after a while – he knew what was going on – so we had to go somewhere else.

I went home to Didcot on Wednesday night just to see my girlfriend and Mum and Dad and to tell them that I would not be home that weekend. When I arrived home I read that there had been another derailment near the main line on the east side, on the morning I had left for Old Oak Common. It had happened at about 7.20am as a train of hoppers was being shunted out of the

North British diesel-hydraulic No 6351 at Didcot in 1965. We were working on a sister loco at Old Oak Common when one of its engines dropped off the lifting hook. *Author*

BACK ON THE RAILS

A newspaper cutting showing one of the derailed hoppers being lifted by the steam crane and breakdown crew from Old Oak Common. The hoppers had been bound for Westbury. *Author's collection*

marshalling yard, so I had been lucky and missed it. Three hopper wagons and a guard's van had come off the road; the hoppers had gone over on their sides, and the Old Oak crane had lifted them back on the road.

The it was back to the grindstone. I caught the train to Reading, then on to Paddington, but as we came alongside Old Oak carriage sidings the train came to a stop. The signals were green and the line ahead was clear. Then four railwaymen opened a door and jumped down onto the track in the middle of the main line. I did the same. Why go into London when the shed was so close? The four waved to the driver of the diesel engine and away went the train. I looked all ways and crossed over, following the four men. They asked me who I was, and I told them that I was like them, an apprentice fitter, so we all walked to the shed together.

I clocked on about 7.15am then went into the locker room to change. In came all the other apprentices, talking together until they saw me. All I said was, 'Late, aren't you?'

They were gob-smacked. 'How the hell did you get in so early?'

I told them, and they couldn't believe what I had done.

My job was servicing the diesel engines of the D1000 'Westerns' in the Pullman shed, working with a fitter called John. We had to

remove the out-of-date fire extinguisher bottles from the inside corner near the diesel engine. These bottles were as tall as an oxygen bottle and as heavy; the halogen gas they contained was used to suffocate the oxygen if an engine-room fire should occur. John and I had to lift them out of the corner, first of all disconnecting the lever and wire attached to them, then making them safe by pushing a pin back into the lever so that they did not explode. We lifted the bottles through a side door near the engine. Like everything else, nothing was planned – you crawled over and climbed over, scraping your fingers, etc. We got both bottles out and refitted two new ones, but as the last one went in and we hooked up the arms and wire it fired off and we both legged it over the diesel engine and out like cats on a hot tin roof. Once again we removed the old bottle and fitted a new one. We were both exhausted.

Each night I made my way home from work to Whitechapel. I travelled with Barry Trim on the Bakerloo line from Willesden Junction. Barry got off at Kensal Green and I changed at Baker Street or Liverpool Street to reach Whitechapel. It was better than going home to Didcot every night. I loved London in the 1960s.

That weekend I was invited to the engagement party of John Langstone and Margaret; like myself and Jen they are still

The remains of Didcot Shed after everything was gone. These are Nos 3 and 4 roads. *Author*

together today. So Barry, the two Scottish lads and I caught the train to Romford for the party on Saturday night. We all had a hell of a night. They found me under a barrel of beer with the tap running and the beer flowing into my mouth and over the floor. I was out for the count. I lost Barry, and we missed the last train home, so we walked back to Acton, about 21 miles. We made it back by Sunday lunchtime.

The work was good at Old Oak and the men and apprentices were pleasant company. I went home the following weekend and swapped my BSA 250cc for a 350cc Triumph motorbike, white with cow-horn handlebars and twin exhaust pipes. I had worked hard for it. It was now December time, and I thought of Bengy – there would be no sing-song in the cabin this year, or any other year.

One day I was sent out by the electrical foreman to marshalling yards in London, as I had been in 1964, the last time I was at Old Oak. This was to check the hour meters on the engines of 350hp diesel-electric shunters, making a note of their numbers, the hours run and their position. Riding around London in a works van with the driver was a sightseeing tour as well.

At Christmas we all went down to Willesden Junction station; there was a pub overlooking the station and Barry, John and I had a good time. 'Blondie' wished everyone a good Christmas and I went home to Didcot. The shed there wasn't a nice sight – the place was nearly dead. Some shunters were there, mostly English Electric 350hp 0-6-0s, but the shed was empty.

7
1966: A FITTER AT OXFORD

I did not go back to work after Christmas as I had in other years, but stayed on holiday till the New Year. On the morning of Saturday 1 January 1966 I rode to Didcot station and heard that there had been another derailment in the same area as the earlier ones, at Foxhall Bridge, where No 7912 *Little Linford Hall* had come to grief in 1961. I therefore rode up to Foxhall and across the bridge, then rode down the embankment to the point where the path ended, so I could get as close as possible. I waved to the fitters from Old Oak and they called me over to the breakdown van. They had been called out early that morning, as the train had come off the tracks at about 1.30am; it was a Sulzer diesel engine pulling a mixed train of coal wagons and box vans from Severn Tunnel Junction to Bletchley. We were having a joke about something when 'Legs' (Mr Diamond) appeared and I asked if I could help out, as all the rest of the crew wanted me there. He agreed, so I went home and changed into my work clothes, telling Mum where I was and that I would see her on Sunday night. I also called at the Co-Op to tell Jen.

Back at the derailment it was a good experience, slinging the chains onto the wreckage and lifting. The Swindon crane come in close and was pulling the coal trucks away from the main line and lifting them onto the embankment. The locomotive had jumped the points and crashed onto its side, embedding itself in the ground, and about 20 coal wagons and box vans had jumped over the engine. The rest of the wagons had crashed into each other and the wreckage was spread onto the main line. Coal was thrown everywhere and the goods wagons were piled sky-high on top of each other. The locomotive was the last thing to be lifted after all the wagons. The driver and second man (fireman) were badly shocked but unhurt, and the guard was taken to hospital in Oxford with a shoulder injury. The Oxford line was clear, but the Paddington to Swindon line was closed to traffic and trains were diverted.

We worked all day and into the night helping to move the wreckage. Hot food was brought in and some was cooked in the breakdown vans, while tea and coffee flowed to keep us warm. As darkness fell lamps were switched on around the wreckage. I remember that a couple of men were not able to get onto the top wagon to rig up the chains to make a lift, so I held onto the chains and was lifted up on top, where I attached the chains. I climbed down by ladder and the lift was made. Once the pile got lower it became easier to reach the other wreckage. Both cranes worked together all night to get a line clear so that passenger trains could slowly pass. All the wagons were write-offs and were sent for scrap.

By Sunday the wreckage had been cleared away, then the lift of the diesel engine was made. Both cranes, one at each end, lifted together – what a sight! 'Legs' Diamond sent me home exhausted, and all the men said that they would see me on Monday. I went to bed after a hot bath.

There followed a spate of derailments. The

Above The Brush Type 4 on its side near Foxhall signal box, 1 January 1966. *R. J. Russell*

Below The smashed bodies of the wagons lifted to one side ready to be picked up later. *R. J. Russell*

Swindon crane itself came off the track near Steventon on its way home, but they were fortunate – being a breakdown crew, they put themselves back on the track! On 7 January there was another derailment at Uffington on the Swindon line. A mixed good train of 52 wagons, including 12 wagons carrying heavy metal slabs, derailed and ripped up the sleepers; it had come from Acton in West London and was on its way to Port Talbot in South Wales. This time the track-laying gangs came in to remove the old track and lay new; they worked through the weekend to get the main line open for the earliest time possible.

On Monday morning, back at Old Oak, I said nothing about the weekend working on the breakdown. But at mid-morning break at 10.00am I was approached by John Langstone

Left The fourth derailment in 11 days occurred at Uffington between Didcot and Swindon on 7 January 1966. This newspaper cutting shows the sleepers smashed by the train, which was carrying ingots and iron ore. *Author's collection*

Below The 20-ton Old Oak Common steam breakdown crane was built by Cowans & Sheldon, and had its own trailing wagon. *Derek Everson*

and was called a scabby creep, and when the word got out about what I had done, all the apprentices were choked. I was called into Mr Diamond's office and thanked, and also told I had the retainer plus the overtime rate and any other payment he could get his hands on. Thanks, 'Legs'!

Meanwhile work was the same old thing, servicing 'Westerns' in the Pullman shed, and going out to marshalling yards checking the engine hour meters on shunters for the Electrical Foreman. I would always end up at Battersea Power Station yard. I always enjoy that part of London.

On Fridays I caught the empty carriages from the sidings up to Paddington at 4.00pm and sat in the same spot when the diesel engine got coupled up at the station till we reached Didcot; or if a Didcot crew was driving the diesel, I would get into the cab up front with them. On Saturday mornings I got up early and went down to the 'Buccaneer' on my 350cc Triumph 'T90' motorbike, and see Jen at Blewbury.

Late afternoon Sunday I caught the train back to London, and sat opposite a chap about the same age as me, and we talked about this and that. The carriage was fairly empty and there were just the two of us in the compartment. He asked where I worked, and as we passed the clock opposite Old Oak Common carriage sidings I pointed out the shed and said that I was an apprentice fitter there. I then asked what he did. He said he was a singer and was off to London to make a name for himself. He said his name was Donovan.

We said our goodbyes at Paddington and I caught the Underground to Whitechapel for another week 'up in the smoke' on the Great

My 1965 Privilege Underground ticket from Willesden Junction. *Author's collection*

My 350cc Triumph Tiger 90. *Author*

Western Railway. My aunt and uncle asked me if I would be staying with them or would I be out and about 'all over Acton with your mates again'? I gave them my lodging money and said that I would see them that night, but I was out every night with the Scottish lads partying and I slept on the hostel floor a few times that week. But I was never late for work the next day.

On Monday morning someone had clocked me in at 7.30am and I walked in at 8.00am. The time clerk was at the clock, and all I could say was that I didn't know who had done it. I was let go, but I collared the chap who clocked me in and asked him not to do it again. Next morning the same thing happened. I was marched into Mr Diamond's office and again said that I didn't know who it was. Next day there was a letter attached to my card telling me to report to Mr Diamond's office at once. I thought, 'Here we go again!' I thought I was due for the biggest telling-off of all time.

But no – I was told that I was to go to work

at Southall, Slough, Reading and Didcot checking axles with a test engineer, carrying all the equipment for both of us. The idea was that we were to put a low-frequency ultrasound signals through the front axles of DMUs, then read the scope to see if the front

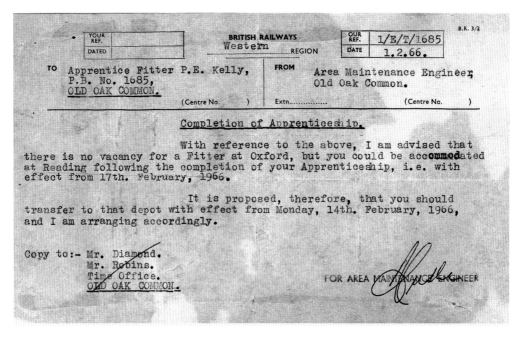

| YOUR REF. | | | BRITISH RAILWAYS | | OUR REF. | 1/E/T/1685 | B.R. 3/2 |
| DATED | | | Western REGION | | DATE | 1.2.66. | |

TO Apprentice Fitter P.E. Kelly,
P.B. No. 1685,
OLD OAK COMMON.

FROM Area Maintenance Engineer,
Old Oak Common.

(Centre No.   )   Extn...............   (Centre No.   )

Completion of Apprenticeship.

      With reference to the above, I am advised that there is no vacancy for a Fitter at Oxford, but you could be accommodated at Reading following the completion of your Apprenticeship, i.e. with effect from 17th. February, 1966.

      It is proposed, therefore, that you should transfer to that depot with effect from Monday, 14th. February, 1966, and I am arranging accordingly.

Copy to:- Mr. Diamond.
          Mr. Robins.
          Time Office.
          OLD OAK COMMON.

FOR AREA MAINTENANCE ENGINEER

On completion of my apprenticeship in February 1966 it was proposed that I move to Reading, but luckily I got what I wanted – a job at Oxford shed. *Author's collection*

| YOUR REF. | | | BRITISH RAILWAYS | | OUR REF. | 1/E/T/1685 | B.R. 3/2 |
| DATED | | | Western REGION | | DATE | 2.2.66. | |

TO Apprentice Fitter P.E. Kelly,
P.B. No. 1685,
OLD OAK COMMON.

FROM Area Maintenance Engineer,
Old Oak Common.

(Centre No.   )   Extn...............   (Centre No.   )

Completion of Apprenticeship.

      Further to my letter of yesterday, I am now advised that there will be a vacancy at Oxford as from 17th. February and in this connection, it is now proposed that you should transfer to that Depot and NOT Reading as previously advised, on Monday, 14th. February, 1966.

      Will you kindly note.

FOR AREA MAINTENANCE ENGINEER

axles or driving wheels were cracked or flawed. We had to remove the bearing casings at both ends and wipe off the grease, attach wires from the axle to the ultrasound scope box, then send a small charge through the axle. If the line on the scope 'wiggled' it would indicate a crack, but if it was straight it was OK. I was out until February, touring the Western Region and learning something at last. All the findings were reported back to work, then any cracked or flawed axles were replaced in the workshops.

On the first Tuesday of February 1966 there was a memo attached to my clock card, again asking me to report to 'Legs'. He asked me where I wanted to go when my apprenticeship was completed, and I said Oxford shed. He phoned through, but unfortunately there was no chance of a move there. He therefore asked me to stay at Old Oak, but I declined as the travelling was too much – but I do wish I had stayed. A move to Reading was proposed, but he said he would help me out somehow to get where I wanted to work.

The following morning I was again called into Mr Diamond's office and he handed me another memo – he had got me the transfer I wanted. I thanked him for everything he had done, and he thanked me for the work I had carried out for the depot. He was a good old boy.

I had two weeks left at Old Oak, so that day I took John Langstone over to the carriage sidings works to look for a chap called Paddy with whom I had been at Swindon in the welding training school. I introduced him to John and we swapped stories about the apprentice whose motorcycle magazine we had put in the box and welded it up. We all had a laugh about it, then I shook hands with Paddy and wished him luck.

I was next told that in a couple of days I was to go out on a test run on a D1000 'Western' Class diesel-hydraulic. We got clearance to be allowed out onto the main line, which was clear down to West Drayton, so we undertook speed trials to test the engine's revs, taking readings in the engine room while on the move.

During my last couple of days I went over to Whitechapel and said my goodbyes to my aunt

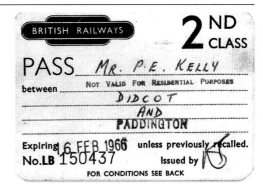

My last workman's pass from Didcot to Paddington. *Author's collection*

and uncle. Then I went out with the lads for a booze-up to say our own goodbyes. I was called into Mr Diamond's office, we shook hands and he handed my indentures as a time-served Maintenance Fitter and Turner. Sometimes I wish I had stayed at Old Oak Common – it was the best place to be stationed.

●

I started work at Oxford at 8 o'clock on the morning of Monday 14 February 1966. I left Didcot station that morning with Paddy Driscoll on the 7.10am, and we got to Oxford at about 7.45am, having stopped at the intermediate stations, Appleford Halt, Culham and Radley. We walked together off the north end of the platform to the path that followed the railway line over the bridge and the River Isis, then into the side shed over the roads, looking all ways for any locomotive movements.

I had to report to Bill Miles, the Foreman of the Running & Maintenance Department. His office was straight through the Fitting Shop, and he welcomed me to the depot and told me what my duties and work times would be while I worked there. I was also told that Paddy was going to be my mate.

So the first week I was shown the ropes and did a few repairs on an English Electric 350hp diesel shunter. They had a few there for the marshalling yards at Hinksey and another yard up near the station. Oxford was a small shed, and at that time was being thinned out; some

Above 2-8-0T No 7239 approaches Oxford General station from the south in the early 1960s. The photograph was taken from Oxford Station South signal box. *R. J. Russell*

Left Ex-LMS No 45331 leaves Oxford with a passenger train on 3 March 1966. *Author*

steam shunting engines were still in operation, but they were few and far between.

Near the coal stage there was a line of scrap engines waiting to be cut up and sent away. Later, when there was no work, this is what I had to do. But at the moment I was concerned with the day-to-day running of the shed. The manpower was next to nothing, and if I had known this I would have gone to Reading depot to work. But I was here, so there it was. There was one Fitter on nights, one on afternoons, and Brian Scarrat on days. Nights were 10.00pm till 8.00am and days were 8.00am till 5.00pm. We had to work six nights, starting on Sunday through to a Saturday morning finish.

In the Fitting Shop there was a lathe, a drill and a grindstone, all running off a system of drive belts. There was also a forge and welding area, with a set of bottles, oxygen and acetylene, for cutting. In the middle of the shop was a desk with a workbook, in which we wrote what work was done daily and on all shifts.

When I started the three Fitters had it sewn up that they would have every bank holiday off and also rest days, but I had to work mine. It seemed it was all done fairly, but I didn't think so at the time.

On the Sunday at the end of my first week, 20 February, I started nights, and somehow I knew it was going to be a hell of a week. Paddy Driscoll lived at the bottom of Sinodun Road, and at about 8.30pm he waited for me to ride down to meet him. Then we both went down to the station and left our bikes in the parcels office under the tunnel opposite the ticket office. We then walked up to the platform and caught the 9.00pm train to Oxford, which got in at about 9.25pm. Walking out of the station, we went into the White House pub opposite the taxi rank. We had to be on duty at 10.00pm, so we had a couple of pints of beer each, then walked down to the shed and signed on.

The work wasn't much: pack a piston gland, grease up a diesel shunter or fill a diesel's tanks for the driver next morning. I couldn't sleep, although Paddy got his head down. I walked the shed, which wasn't as nice as Didcot; in fact, it was totally different, with ashes and dirt and filth everywhere.

As morning came I looked across the main line to the church to see what time it was: 4.00am. Then I walked north up the main line towards Wolvercote, about 1½-2 miles from the shed, came back and woke Paddy, as he wanted to finish early and catch the 6.00am train home to Didcot. We agreed that I would see him the same time that night. I always liked nights, but I hated the 2.00-10.00pm shifts, the afternoons.

Paddy got away and I wasn't far behind him at about 7.30am. When the day-shift Fitter came in I legged it to catch my train at 7.40am. I was crossing the bridge over the River Isis when I heard a steam locomotive approaching behind me with a mixture of box vans and coal wagons. I got to the crossing between the platforms when the loco whistle blew and the driver hung out of the cab – it was Fred Jones ('Old Man River') on a 'Hall' Class locomotive. He was waving and shouting at me: 'I can't stop, but hop on!'

So I slung my lunch bag over my shoulder and climbed up onto the footplate as the train was moving.

'I couldn't stop,' said Fred, 'because we got the all clear to go first before the passenger from the station will leave.'

Then he opened up the regulator. All I heard was the vans banging and the couplings cracking buffer to buffer and knocking. I thought of the guard in his van. I bet he was raging when Fred pulled away. We got out of the station and were soon well on our way.

Fred said, 'I'll drop you opposite the station at Didcot on the east loop line, as we're going on to Reading.'

As we came into Radley Fred called me over to him; I was standing on the fallplate between the locomotive and tender looking over the side at what we were pulling, and partly in a dream. He shouted, 'Move *now!*' so I walked over to him and said, 'What's wrong?'

'Look at the fallplate,' he said. At Radley there was a curve banked away from the station and the tender was moving and twisting from side to side relative to the loco footplate; I had never seen anything like it. Fred had saved my life – I would have had my legs cut off at the ankles!

We had a hell of a run up to the signal on the loop line at Didcot. I was pleased because I had ridden a locomotive pulling a train, and also because I had never been on the east loop line heading towards Reading. I climbed down and walked across the roads to the station, jumped up onto the platform, down the stairs to the parcels office for my bike, then home to bed, after having met my girlfriend at the bottom of Hagbourne Bridge. I did the same thing for the rest of the week until Friday night.

An Oxford-bound Southern 'Pacific' approaches Radley station in 1962. *Author*

On Friday we caught the train as usual at 9.00pm for the night shift, and went into the White House again to have a drink. We both knew we had caught up with the workload and there was not much to do, just odds and ends. So Paddy rang down to the shed and told the Foreman that, if he wanted us, to ring the pub, and also could he sign us both on? He agreed, so we had a few pints each, then a few more. We went back to work happy as two sandboys. Paddy passed out in the Fitters' cabin, but I couldn't sleep – well, no one let me sleep. When locomotives moved along the roads in and around the shed the rails went up and down, and as the steam shunting engine, an 0-6-0 Pannier tank, went to move over some points it jumped off the road. The lines were just kept together by coal, ash and grease – in the time I spent there I never saw a sleeper between the Fitting Shop and the Fitters' cabin.

I tried to wake Paddy to give me a hand, but he was comatose. With the help of the Shed Foreman and the fireman we pulled the traversing jacks from the breakdown van, which was close by, and some blocks of wood. We put the wood under the front of the loco with the traverse jack, and worked the engine back over onto the road, but then the other end started to swing off the road. I went under the frame and wheels and slipped some blocks of wood between the points and the wheels, leaving the jacks under the front. The Shed Foreman said that it wouldn't work, the whole lot would come off, and if it did we would be there all night. I asked the fireman to drive back slowly, which he did. The back wheels stayed on the line and the front dropped back on as I let the jack down – the 'tanky' was back on the road. I thanked Paddy for his help…

I was also asked to check out a steam loco's smokebox door, but when I climbed up onto the front I tripped and fell off onto the floor. It was a good job I didn't hurt myself. I soon sobered up and climbed back up to complete the job.

At the end of the shift we went home for a long weekend till Monday afternoon. Then it

Oxford Shed on 5 March 1966. The Fitters' cabin can be seen on the left, while the large building in the background is the Lifting or Fitting Shop, which was dirty and dingy and not looked after like Didcot's shed. On the right is a Brush Type 4 on standby for the breakdown van in case of derailment. The set of points to the left of the diesel is where the 'tanky' came off the track early one morning when I was working nights. *Author*

was the afternoon shift, 2.00pm till 10.00pm, and what a horrible shift that was! Afternoons were a drag; I caught the 12.30pm train from Didcot to Oxford and returned home in the evening on the last train at 9.50pm, by which time there was no one about.

I came into work one afternoon to start my shift, and had drawn the short straw again – I had to change the brake blocks on an 0-6-0 'tanky' in the Fitting Shop. Everybody had gone home; just Paddy and I were left in the shed. Then a Paddington express came in; it was not scheduled to stop at Oxford, but the traction unit of the 'Hymek' was experiencing fuel trouble. This was an emergency, as there was a huge risk of fire. The Shedmaster told me that he would get the standby diesel fired up with a crew ready in case I needed it. The signal box was informed what was about to happen, and the standby diesel, a D63xx Class diesel, went out up the relief line to the station.

I was waiting at the top end of the platform as the passenger train came in. As I climbed into the cab the driver was on his way out – I was surprised that he stank of diesel. I went into the diesel compartment and it was totally covered in fuel. It was so bad that if a spark came off the engine it would have exploded. The main fuel injector pipe had split. I was only in the engine for 10-15 minutes but my clothes stank to high heaven of fuel.

I told the Station Master that I was having the diesel engine shut down and moved off the coaches because of the risk of fire. We waved to the signalman to change the points to bring in the standby, which was waiting on the up relief line. The D63xx duly came in and pulled the 'Hymek' into the sidings. Then it came back onto the passenger train, coupled up and was ready to pull out, but in the meantime a man in a pin-striped suit approached me. He said he was going to report me for hanging around, even though it had all been done

'Western' Class diesel-hydraulic No D1047 *Western Lord* awaiting repairs on Oxford shed in 1966. Next to it is a Brush Type 4. *Author*

within 40 minutes. I told him to spell my name correctly – there was only one 'e' in Kelly.

The train went on its way and I rang the Shedmaster for a second diesel to come in and pull the 'Hymek' back to the shed. We let it cool down, then rang Reading depot to get a new fuel injector pipe sent for the day shift to fit.

The next time I came on shift Paddy and I had to change the halogen bottle in a 'Western' Class diesel; the roof plates were taken off for easier access. The rest of the week was normal except I ran out of work, so I had to pull the cutting gear and a set of oxygen and acetylene bottles up to the coal stage where the steam locomotives were being kept for scrap. It was shameful: a line of dead steam locomotives with their nameplates and numberplates gone.

Picking a locomotive that had not been touched, I torched the con-rods and piston rods away from the crossheads, then put them up in the tenders to go. In all, there were three

roads of dead locomotives waiting to be taken away to be scrapped. Diesels would take four or maybe five locomotives at a time up to Barry in Wales to the scrapyards, and a few went to other destinations, such as the National Coal Board.

Among them was No 6984 *Owsden Hall*, minus name and numberplates. In all, 330 'Halls' and 'Modified Halls' had been built, and the GWR took the names for most of them from three reference books, the first of which was a list of stately homes that opened their gardens to the public occasionally each year, generally to raise money for charity. However, when a spelling mistake appeared in the book, the mistake also appeared on the locomotive nameplate!

The 'Manor' names came from a similar source, with a long list of names that were noted for future locomotives that were never built. The first batch was to have been of 40 locomotives, but the Second World War put a stop to the second 20, so the names only ran from A to H. The other names, which

Top No 6984 *Owsden Hall*, minus name and numberplates, waits at Oxford to be scrapped. Note the missing connecting rod. *Author*

Middle and bottom Two views of the coaling stage locomotives awaiting their fate at Oxford on 5 March 1966. *Author*

had been selected in 1937, were as follows: 7820 *Henley Manor*, 7821 *Hughenden Manor*, 7822 *Huntley Manor*, 7823 *Ofton Manor*, 7824 *Kenfig Manor*, 7825 *Leckwith Manor*, 7826 *Liddington Manor*, 7827 *Membury Manor*, 7828 *Marden Manor*, 7829 *Newnham Manor*, 7830 *Norton Manor*, 7831 *Ogwell Manor*, 7832 *Pimley Manor*, 7833 *Ramsbury Manor*, 7834 *Rodley Manor*, 7835 *Standen Manor*, 7836 *Sutton Manor*, 7837 *Thorton Manor*, 7838 *Widford Manor*, and 7839 *Wilcote Manor*. Only *Ramsbury Manor* was re-chosen after the war.

The GWR did not seem to appreciate that a 'Manor' was an area of land allocated to a particular noble lord in Norman times, who became 'Lord of the Manor', but he did not have to build a Manor House upon his land, and many did not. For instance, Cookham Manor, the name carried by No 7808, was just open land including Winter Hill and

Left On the same day a 'Hall' 4-6-0 waits to be towed away. *Author*

Below With the con-rods and crosshead also gone, 2-6-2T No 6132 is ready to be hauled away on 5 March 1966. I am being helped by young apprentice fitter John Clanfield. His father was a Fitter's mate working in Didcot shed near the end of steam. *Author*

Pinkneys Green. The Lord of the Manor was entitled to hunt the deer in Windsor Great Park up to seven times a year, but woe betide him if he tried the eighth time! Odney has a Manor House, but it is called Lullebrook Manor, not Odney. *Draycott Manor* (No 7810) should have been *Draycot Manor*, and *Granville Manor* (No 7818) should really have been *Grenville Manor*. Swindon did seem to make rather a mess of the 'Manor' names.

Many of the name and numberplates were disposed of to enthusiasts for a few shillings. There's a story about a dentist in the North West who had his surgery near the engine shed. He was very keen on the stories about the Great Western Railway that the drivers and firemen told him while he was extracting or filling their teeth. He would even give free treatment in return for the railway tales. When the time came for the dentist to retire to North Wales, the shed staff wanted to show their appreciation. They told him to be at the station when a particular express train came through as they had something for him; he still did a little postal business in false teeth, so expected it was some materials he had ordered. The loco hauling the train was a 'Manor', and the Shed Foreman looked the other way while someone loosened the bolts from behind one of the nameplates before leaving the shed to couple up to the coaches.

Once under way the fireman climbed out and walked along the side of the 'Manor', holding on for dear life. As the driver slowed the train slightly, the fireman removed the nameplate then climbed back into the cab They wrapped the nameplate in sacking, tied it up with string and labelled it with the dentist's name. As the train approached the station the driver slowed right down. The gentleman was waiting right on time expecting teeth, but the fireman threw the nameplate into a bush next to him, then the driver opened up the regulator to gather speed again.

The Shed Foreman demanded to know what had become of the nameplate. The crew said that it must have become loose and had fallen off somewhere during the journey. In fact, the Foreman knew perfectly well what had happened and what had been done. The name of the 'Manor' is not known.

Paddy and I finished our afternoons that week and were due to return on days, thank God. I looked forward to days because I could get out in the evenings; I hated afternoons because it was boring and you saw no one when you got home, just bath and bed. In the mornings everyone was at work. Paddy and I caught the train to Oxford at 12.30pm, arriving at about 1.00pm. We went into the buffet bar on the station and have a few pints, then walked down to the shed to work it off.

About this time there was another derailment at Didcot's north-end marshalling yard, where the petrol train had caught fire, involving a collision between two freight trains. At about 5.45am the 2.25am Banbury to Sonning coal train was being shunted into the yard with about 26 wagons unhitched. Because of the slight gradient in the yard a few of the wagons and the guard's van ran backwards into the Banbury-Aldermaston freight waiting to come into the yard at the north end. Seven wagons and the guard's van were derailed.

The rush-hour Didcot to Oxford passenger service suffered the most because it was not possible to run trains into Didcot station from Oxford without reversing them from Didcot East Junction. The Old Oak Common crane and breakdown crews were called to retrieve the train and put the wagons back on the line. As I passed the scene on my way to Oxford I saw one of the Fitters who had been an apprentice at Old Oak. My DMU was slowly going by, so I shouted out to him, 'Tell Barry and John to call me!' He had blond hair but I forget his name.

Consequently I had a surprise during the week when John Langstone, Barry Hughes and the chap I saw at the derailment scene got permission to leave Old Oak and drove up to Oxford shed. We all went down to the White House, sank a few pints and had a good talk and a laugh. That was the last time I saw John till … but that's another story.

I had a good week on days, then on Saturday and Sunday morning John Clanfield helped me change a set of brake shoes on an 0-6-0 'tanky' in the Lifting Shop. This was the last steam engine I recall working on. Oxford was being run down and the best locomotives had gone.

Oxford Shed, 5 March 1966: the breakdown van is behind the 'tanky', with the Lifting Shop beyond. *Author*

Paddy and I had nights again for six nights, most of the work being cutting up steam locomotives in the back of the shed under cover amongst all the ashes and dirt – no one ever cleaned up. We also filled diesel shunters ready for their morning jobs in the yards, and signed off the work sheet.

●

Burton Agnes Hall is a 17th-century house near the seaside town of Bridlington in North Yorkshire. The gardens with their maze have been featured on television on several occasions, while the house, with its Great Hall and many carvings, contains treasures of French art by Renoir, Gauguin and many more. The house was built by the Boynton family in 1610, and later its priceless antiques were inherited by a young boy, left to him by a bachelor cousin, 85-year-old Marcus Wickham-Boynton; he inherited £10 million plus the estate, and was now the Lord of the 380-year-old estate, with his own butler.

This famous name was later bestowed on Great Western Railway 'Modified Hall' Class 4-6-0 No 6998, built at Swindon Works and completing her trials on 28 January 1949. She cost £8,500 to build, including her boiler at £2,262; the tender was an extra £2,035. She weighed 122 tons 10 cwt and 63ft 0¼in long.

The locomotive had a series of tenders over the years, all of which held 4,000 gallons of water:

Year	Tender No
1949	4077
1951	2647
1954	2914
1955	2758
1958	2765
1961	2394
1962	2449
1963	4078

All were Collett designs except the last, which was a Hawksworth flat-sided type, unpopular with firemen.

She was allocated to Cardiff shed from 1949 to 1958, Shrewsbury (1958-59), Tyseley (1959-60), Goodwick (1960-61), Old Oak Common (1961-62) and Southall (1963-65). She received regular attention in several workshops then, before leaving to go to Southall, she went back to Swindon for her last overall. Her mileage in 1964 was more than 554,900 miles.

The final end of steam on the GWR came on 3 January 1966. On that day the last train to pull out of Oxford behind a steam locomotive was the 2.20pm service to York, and the loco concerned, specially cleaned for the event, was No 6998 *Burton Agnes Hall*, which took the train only as far as Banbury. Driver Gerry Faulkener and his fireman, Pat Cook, brought the locomotive out of Oxford shed, with Reginald Hanks, Chairman of the Western Region, also on the footplate. Seeing her off from the down platform at Oxford was the Lord Mayor of Oxford, Alderman Mrs Kathleen Lower, with her hand on the regulator, a moment that brought back memories of all the many locomotives that had travelled so many miles through the years.

When *Burton Agnes Hall* returned to the shed at Oxford, she left on the up relief from Oxford to Didcot, where she was sold direct to the Great Western Society Ltd in running order. She stayed over at Didcot, then went down to Totnes in April 1966. In December 1967 she left there for her new home at Didcot engine shed.

●

I have kept the following events to myself for more than 40 years. I was on days with Paddy, and two other Fitters were on afternoons, plus one working a rest day. The two Fitters wanted to set fire to the breakdown van; they poured paraffin over everything in the van and told me to keep an eye open. I refused to be part of it. They were subsequently caught, and blamed me.

I was taken in the office and told I was going to be sacked by the Area Maintenance Engineer, Mr Perry. I told Paddy what had happened and went off to do a job. Mr Perry called me into his office and said he was sorry what had happened. He told me that Paddy Driscoll had been to see him and had told him what had happened and had stood up for me. He had also spoken about the other two and what was going on.

On 15 June, because of what had happened, I decided to resign from the railway, and now, writing this book, I feel the truth has to come out. I was ashamed to be blamed by the manager when I had told the truth all the time. So I made a story up that I couldn't get on with the shift work and wished to leave the railway.

I resigned on 24 June 1966.

Below My final three-monthly workman's pass between Didcot and Oxford. *Author's collection*

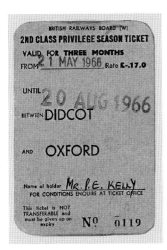

Right The acknowledgement of my resignation from Area Maintenance Engineer Mr Perry. *Author's collection*

British Railways Western Region

Fitter. P.Kelly   Area Maintenance Dept

Running & Maintenance Dept   Oxford

Oxford

y/r
o/r 2/1/66   Date   15.6.66

Resignation from the Service
24.6.66

Although I, personally have only had the post of Area Maintenance Engineer at Oxford for a short while, and therefore have not a very lengthy knowledge of you , I feel I should not let you leave the Service without thanking you for the work you have done.

I understand that your new post does not call for shift work, the reason you are leaving us.

May I wish you every success in your new employment.

D A J Perry

Area Maintenance Engineer

8
REUNIONS

In 1973 my wife Jen and I and our first daughter Lisa went to the Didcot Railway Society on their open day. We were standing near to where the carriage sidings used to be, from the crossover from the shops out of the tunnel under the station. A steam locomotive was pulling a set of carriages alongside us and the driver, Harry Merrick, and his fireman, Tony Neal, leaned out of the side window of

the cab and asked me to come up on the footplate and have a ride. Jen declined the offer, but I climbed up onto the footplate and was asked whether I would I like to drive the locomotive. It was 'Hall' Class No 6998 *Burton Agnes Hall*. The last time I had seen her had been coming into Didcot station on the up relief from Oxford in December 1965.

A man was filming the event, standing on top of the coal in the tender. I wound the gear lever into reverse and released the vacuum brake, pulled the whistle chain with one hell of a pull and got the all clear from Tony Neal, who was looking for the green flag from the guard.

Then it happened. I opened the regulator wide open and she drove her wheels round and round and black smoke jetted out through the chimney. Everybody around the locomotive jumped up and down with excitement, except Harry. I shut the regulator, and stood grinning at Harry. Then I opened up the regulator slowly to allow the wheels to grip the rails, blew the whistle and away we drove down to the blocks, passing the old Fitting Shop and bringing back memories, as well as a small tear to my eye.

The guard waved his red flag and Tony said, 'OK, slow up,' so I applied the vacuum brake a little at a time to slow us down and bring us to a stop.

Preserved ex-GWR 4-6-0 No 6998 *Burton Agnes Hall* runs along the up relief from Oxford at Didcot station. She was the last steam locomotive from Oxford shed. *Author*

I wound the lever into forward gear. Harry looked at me as if to say, 'Don't you dare – not again!' But like a good boy I blew the whistle, let off the vacuum brake and away we went back up to where we started.

I stopped the locomotive, blew the whistle again for old times' sake – the emergency brake whistle – just to hear it again. I then shook hands with both men and got off the footplate.

But when I got down to rejoin the family I got a hell of a telling-off. They were covered in black smuts. However, the man filming got off the tender and shook my hand; he was over the moon and said that what I had done had made his day.

I didn't see Harry Merrick or Tony Neal again till 2000/01 when we all met up in the Railway Staff Club in Didcot, with the remark from Ted Rock, 'Here comes one of the "Family of Fitters".' People who do not forget choke me up.

●

In 1999 I wrote a six-page letter to Ed Stewart's 'Where are you now?' show on BBC Radio 2, explaining that we had worked at Old Oak Common between 1963 and 1965. I told him that we had been apprentices together on British Railways. I also told him where John got engaged and to whom. Barry had gone on to work at Heathrow Airport.

On 26 March, after the programme went out on the air, I had a letter back from Barry, who lived in Bracknell. I rang him but there was no reply, so Jen and I got into the car and drove to his home, but he was away. I put a note through his door saying who I was and was he a 'cockney from Acton'? I also left my phone number and my address; I lived in the Northampton area at that time. The following week Jen and I were invited down to his home. We were both older, but we could hardly get a word in edgeways, we talked so much. It was like walking back into 1965 again – I couldn't believe it – although Barry was a lot broader, like me. His wife is Maretta, and how lovely she is!

Barry had John's telephone number and I rang him; John and Margaret came up to see us in August 1999. He too had not changed a bit.

I wrote again to the Ed Stewart show on Radio 2 and said we had met, but not yet all together as a party. I am working on it. I keep in touch with John and Margaret with Christmas cards and phone calls, and we will come together, I know it. Barry sometimes rings me; he says that I managed to find those two, and we shall never lose touch again.

Something else came out of all this. Derek Everson knew me in 1964 at Old Oak Common, but I did not see him in 1965. We keep in touch; he and Barry work together at Heathrow, and Derek gave me a lot of the Old Oak photos.

People in the town where I lived at the time heard the Ed Stewart show and never realised that I once worked on the old Great Western Railway.

Meanwhile Bengy had gone on to complete his 35 years' service on the railway and collected his long service medal. He had followed me to Oxford shed when I left in June 1966 and he stayed for about a year, then went on. He saw many things happen in Oxford – even someone trying to commit suicide. He and Matt Oglesby, who worked in the permanent way gang, walked up the station together to the London-bound platform and Bengy saw a woman kneeling down across the track; she had a postman's coat on. The train came in with carriages from Worcester; the locomotive and first coach ran past her but only knocked her sideways. Matt said to Bengy to see if her head was still on; Bengy climbed under the first coach in between the carriages and saw that her head was cut but her big toes were cut off. She was knocked out cold.

The Shedmaster told Bengy to pull her out and let the train leave on time, but he declined to do so. In the meantime Bengy sent Matt up to the signal box to phone for an ambulance and requested the Shedmaster to ask on the station tannoy if there was a doctor about. The railway police came and Bengy went to leave them to take over. Their reply was that he was doing OK and should stay with the lady, who in the meantime had woken up. Bengy was sweating icicles – he didn't like it one bit, he told me. The ambulance drove over the main lines and the crew got her out and took her to Oxford Hospital. Bengy said he had a strong cup of sweet tea to help him recover from the shock. Apparently three months later she attempted suicide by jumping off a bridge. I think she might have got her wish.

After that Bengy got a transfer to Plymouth Shed, and he and Marion still live in Cornwall. I hoped that we would see each other after all these years; as the years have gone on we have both got more sensible! Then in July 2002 my wife and I drove to Cornwall for a holiday, found Marion and Bengy and had our reunion.

Barry lost Maretta to cancer a few years ago and he sold up and moved to Spain; we still keep in touch. I also still keep in touch with Tony Neal and Sheila, John and Margaret,

and Bengy and Marion. Mick Howard passed away in 2007; it broke my heart that he never saw retirement.

In 2001 Jen and I moved to Norfolk to retire together. On 13 June 2006 I drove to Didcot from Norfolk to try and find Jimmy Tyler. I found his name and address in the phone book. I went up to the door and knocked it. I heard all the bolts and locks being undone, then the door opened; it seemed that it hadn't been opened for a long time. A little man stood there looking at me. I asked him if Mr Tyler lived there. He then spoke, and I new it was him from his Hereford Welsh accent. We said our hellos then spoke about the times we were on the railway and memories of when I was stationed at Didcot shed. I turned my head to the side slightly and he said, 'You just look like your Dad – you're the image of him.' That brought back memories to me.

Jim said that he would be 91 next year, but he still had his marbles and was quick with it. He remembered when he was my Fitter and how through the years I worked with him he put me right. 'Well, I tried,' he said, 'but you always went your own way.' I stood there, my mind working, and, yes, he was right. If only we could go back again and do things differently! He told me that I was the only one that had ever got in touch over the years. We shook hands, and Jim put his other hand over mine; it was as hard as a rock through all those years doing heavy work. Then as we said our goodbyes the tears rolled from both of our eyes.

I was grateful for the help he gave me in putting this book together. I can still see him today, not the man he was, but the man he is today. My Fitter at Didcot Lifting Shop on the old Great Western Railway.

Jenny and Pat Kelly, July 2000. *Author*

INDEX

Ball, John (fireman) 54

Barlow, Bernard (driver) 57

Bearings, white metal, fitting of new 13-15

Bidmead, Dick (cleaner) 19

'Blondie', apprentice 75, 107

'Blue Pullman' diesel train 77-78, 79, 96

Boilers, washing out of 31

Bourne, E. C. (District Officer) 28

Bradshaw, E. (fireman) 54

Bray, Mrs (time clerk) 11

Braziers ('fire devils') 43, 60

Breakdown trains 26, 27, 28, 34, 47, 65, 68, 72, 90-91, 108, 110, 121; boundaries of operations 57-58

Brinkley, Arthur (workshop foreman) 11, 22, 26, 30, 34, 37, 39, 42, 43, 50, 58, 62, 66, 67, 73, 74, 85, 90, 92, 96

Brown, Alan (apprentice) 71, 74-75

Carter, Keith 'Bengy' (apprentice) 18, 25, 28, 30, 31, 32, 34-35, 38, 39, 42, 43, 47-48, 50, 51, 57, 58, 63, 66, 72, 73, 74, 84, 93, 97, 100, 102, 104, 107, 125-126

Churchill, Sir Winston, funeral train 93-84

Clanfield, John (apprentice) 120, 121

Cook, Pat (fireman) 122

Cooper, Johnny (boilersmith) 42

Curtis, Mrs, landlady 98, 100

Davis, Dai 38

Davis, Dave (fitter) 22, 34, 43, 46, 55-56, 57, 73, 74, 84, 90, 91

Dawson, Cecil 94

Dawson, Cyril (boilersmith) 32, 42

Dearlove, Jack Jnr (fitter) 62, 97

Dearlove, Jack Snr (boilersmith) 42, 62

Derailments 26, 27, 34, 58, 65, 90, 105-106, 108-110, 116, 121; use of jacks 28, 116

Diamond, 'Legs', Chief Mechanical Manager 74, 104, 108, 111, 113

Didcot, origin of railway at 7; fire at station, 1886 7; Parcels Depot/Transfer Shed 39, 63; Provender Stores 51-52; railway hostel 19, 55, 84; sewage works 47-48; wartime at 52

Didcot East Junction 26, 27; North Junction, crashes at 85-87, 90-91

Didcot Ordnance Depot 13, 21, 52, 78, 87

Didcot Railway Staff Club 30, 58-59, 93

Didcot shed 2, 6, 10; ash pan area 12, 31, 45; Christmas at 22-23, 42-43, 59, 73; closure of 93, 95, 101, 102, 107; coaling stage 12, 13, 45; Lifting Shop 11, 13, 14, 15, 16-17, 22, 29, 50, 63, 84-85, 94; locomotive allocations: 1959 10; 1960 21; 1961 40; 1963 61, 72; 1965 103; mess room 30; offices at 11; payday at 90; pedestrian

tunnel into 25-26; reservoir 46; roof refurbishment 96-97; sand furnace 10, 64; staff at, 1960 10; stationary boiler 32-33; turntable 31

Didcot, Newbury & Southampton line 9, 60, 87-90; locos on 89-90

Diesel locomotives: appearance of 66, 98

350hp shunters 72, 107, 113

D63xx' diesel-hydraulics 91, 105, 117

Brush-Sulzer Type 4 75, 78, 108, 109, 117

'Hymek' diesel-hydraulics 66, 67, 71, 100, 117-118

'Warship' diesel-hydraulics 66, 67, 69, 74, 102

'Western' diesel-hydraulics 78-80, 106, 111, 113, 118

Diesel multiple units (DMUs), maintenance of 68-69

Donovan (singer) 111

Dowding, Frank (fitter's mate) 25, 26, 31, 34, 62, 63, 73, 97

Driscoll, Paddy (fitter) 115ff

East, George (shedmaster) 11, 22, 73, 85

Edwards, Tom 93

Everson, Derek 125

Faulkener, Gerry (driver) 122

Fireboxes, working in 62

Fires, lighting in locomotives 31

Fitzgerald, Matt (fireman) 86

Foxhall Junction 35-37, 38; derailments at 34-35, 38, 108-109

Foxhunting 38

Gleason, Mick (firelighter) 31
Gough, Jack (signalman) 27

Hale, Jim (fitter's mate) 57, 73, 84, 91
Hands and skin, cleaning of 25
Hanks, Reginald (Chairman of WR) 122
Holmer, Jim (fitter) 31, 32, 43, 46-47, 51, 55-56, 57, 63, 73, 91, 94
Hopkinson, G. 36
Howard, Mick (apprentice) 38-39, 50, 56, 58-59, 62, 78, 126
Hughes, Barry (apprentice) 75, 80, 104, 107, 121, 125

Ireson, Ted (fireman) 58

James, Roland (fireman) 70-71
Jones, Fred (driver) 115

Kelly, Chris (father) 9, 13, 25, 28, 31, 32, 33-34, 42, 57, 93
Kelly, Paul (brother) 9, 13, 28-29, 50, 51, 55, 73, 84, 87
Kelly, Richard 'Dick' (brother) 9, 13, 25, 50, 68, 87
Knapp, E. (fireman) 54

Langstone, John (apprentice) 75, 80, 104, 106-107, 110, 113, 121, 125, 126
Lazby, Fred (lathe operator) 77, 104
Leaworthy, Arthur (acting shedmaster) 102
Looms, Bob (fitter) 18, 22, 32, 56, 73

Marriner, Mr (labourer) 47
Marshall, Frank (boilersmith) 42
Massey, Mick (apprentice) 67
May, Trevor (boilerman/boiler washer) 13, 31, 32, 33, 42, 57, 93
Merrick, Harry (driver) 70-71, 124-125
Miles, Bill (shed foreman) 113
Mills Hurcol mechanical lubricator 37
Milton, train crash at (1955) 67-68
Moreton marshalling yard 26, 72, 90

Morgan, Sam (office clerk) 22, 58, 74

Neal, Tony (fireman) 124 93, 94, 124-125, 126
Night school 39, 58

Oglesby, Matt (fitter's mate) 32, 47, 50, 63, 73, 94, 125
Old Oak Common shed 34, 74ff, 93, 102, 104ff
Oxford station 114; shed 50, 112, 113ff; Lifting Shop 117, 122

Parson, Jim (storeman) 42
Passey, Burt (fitter) 32
Paul, Ernie 93
Perry, Mr (Area Maintenance Engineer) 123
Phillips, Min (fireman) 59
Piston rings, fitting of new 18, 29-30, 34, 64, 84
Powell, Ted (fitter) 25, 31, 34, 62, 63, 73, 97
Practical jokes 18, 22, 55, 84-85
Preparing locos for duty 64-65

Quartermaine, Mick (apprentice) 71-72, 74-75

Radley station 115, 116
Reading diesel depot 53, 67, 73; turntable 70-71
Royal Train 57
Runaway locomotives 53
Russell, M. (signalman) 26
Russell, Mick (apprentice) 67

Safety valves, removal and refitting of 31-32, 90
Scarrat, Brian (fitter) 115
Shift patterns 28
'Shunt dummy' trucks 50-51
Slip coaches 7-9
Smith, Dave (apprentice) 71-72
Snow, effect of on railway 22, 43-45, 60, 74

Steam locomotives: run-down of 65; scrapping of 41, 80-82, 118, 119, 122; end of steam on ex-GWR 122
0-4-2T 41, 49, 50
0-6-0PTs 12, 21, 34, 39, 42, 76, 81, 116, 122

2-6-0 'Aberdare', used for wartime target practice 42
2-6-0 BR Standard 61
2-8-0 (ex-GWR) 41, 48, 82
2-8-0 (ex-LMS) 8F 83, 86-87
2-8-0 'Austerity' 23, 24
2-10-0 9F 14, 20, 62, 66; *Evening Star* 66, 101
4-4-0 *City of Truro* 56-57
4-6-0 'Castle' 28-30, 46, 54, 65, 81, 82; *Pendennis Castle* 16-17, 77
4-6-0 'Grange' 58, 63-64, 83
4-6-0 'Hall' 13, 14, 19, 20, 32, 33, 34, 40, 47, 70, 90, 93, 94, 103, 115, 118, 119, 120; *Burton Agnes Hall* 122-123, 124
4-6-0 'King' 80, 81; *King George V* 45, 46
4-6-0 'Manor' 70, 101, 118, 120, 121

Strikes 58
Superheaters, replacement of 73
Swindon, lodging in 97; refreshment rooms saga 97-98
Swindon Works 96ff; 'A' Shop 98ff; payday at 99, 101; welding school 100

Tenders and tanks, draining of water 39-40
Tickets and passes 5, 68, 111, 113, 123
Tolly, Cecil (guard) 86
Tools, hand-made 46, 59, 74
Trim, Barry (apprentice) 106
Tyler, Dennis (apprentice) 67, 71-72
Tyler, Jimmy (fitter) 13, 15, 29-30, 32, 37, 43, 53, 56, 63, 66, 68, 72, 84, 85, 94, 126

Ultrasound checking of axles 112-113
Upton station 88

Wallingford 49
Warr, Reg (driver/foreman) 32, 57
Warrick, Bob (fitter's mate) 50, 72
Water troughs and scoops 53, 55
Wheeler, Stan (driver) 86
Woodhouse, Mike (apprentice) 78